Elementa Philoſophica:

Containing chiefly,

NOETICA,

Or THINGS relating to the

Mind *or* Underſtanding:

AND

ETHICA,

Or THINGS relating to the

MORAL BEHAVIOUR.

PHILADELPHIA:
Printed by B. FRANKLIN, and D. HALL, at the *New-Printing-Office*, near the Market. 1752.

KRAUS REPRINT CO.
New York
1969

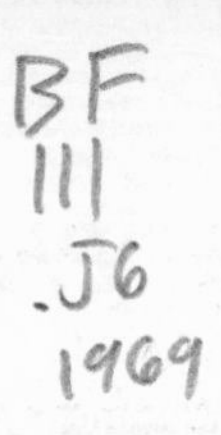

L.C. Catalog Card Number 79-78985

KRAUS REPRINT CO.
A U.S. Division of Kraus-Thomson Organization Limited

Printed in U.S.A.

NOETICA:

OR THE

First PRINCIPLES of KNOWLEDGE,

AND THE

Progress of the *Human Mind*

Towards its

HIGHEST PERFECTION.

NOETICA:

Or the First PRINCIPLES of

Human Knowledge.

BEING A

LOGICK,

Including both

METAPHYSICS and *DIALECTIC*,

Or the ART of REASONING.

With a brief PATHOLOGY, and an Account of the gradual Progress of the HUMAN MIND, from the first Dawnings of Sense to the highest Perfection, both Intellectual and Moral, of which it is capable.

To which is prefixed,

A Short INTRODUCTION

To the

STUDY of the *SCIENCES.*

O Vitæ Philosophia Dux! O Virtutum Indagatrix, Expultrixque Vitiorum! Unus Dies benè, & ex Præceptis tuis actus, peccanti Immortalitati est anteponendus.

CIC. TUSC.

PHILADELPHIA:

Printed by B. FRANKLIN, and D. HALL, at the *New-Printing-Office*, near the Market. 1752.

To the Right REVEREND

Father in GOD,

GEORGE,

Lord Biſhop of *CLOYNE,*

IN

IRELAND;

THE following Eſſay, from the deepeſt Senſe of Gratitude, is moſt humbly inſcribed,

By his Lordſhip's

moſt dutiful and obedient Son,

and moſt obliged humble Servant,

SAMUEL JOHNSON.

ADVERTISEMENT.

AS I am of the Opinion, that little Manuals of the Sciences, if they could be well done, would be of good Use to young Beginners; what I aim at in this little Tract, is to be as useful to them as I can, in the Studies of Metaphysicks *and* Logicks, *and this in order to the more particular Studies of* Nature *and* Morals, *by giving as clear Definitions as I am able in few Words, of the principal Matters and Terms whereof those Studies consist; which I have endeavoured to do, in an Order of Thoughts, gradually arising one after another, in a Manner as instructive as could well be, in so short a Compass. I have also proposed to shew how these Studies, taking their Rise from the first Beginnings of Sense, proceed on through the other Studies, to raise the Mind gradually to its highest Perfection and Happiness.*

THO' I would not be too much attached to any one Author or System, exclusive of any others; yet whoever is versed in the Writings of Bishop Berkeley, *will be sensible that I am in a particular Manner beholden to that excellent Philosopher for several Thoughts that occur in the following Tract. And I cannot but recommend it to any one that would think with Exactness on these Subjects, to peruse all the Works of that great and good Gentleman (as well as those of* Locke, Norris, *or* Malbranch *and* Cambray) *if it were for no other Reason, at least for this, that they will, in the best Manner lead him to think closely, and to think for himself. And I was the rather willing to publish this* Logick, *because I think* Metaphysicks *a necessary Part of that Science, and that I apprehend it a great Damage to the Sciences that the old* Metaphysicks

taphysicks *are so much neglected, and that they might be rendered the more pleasant and useful by joining with them some Improvements of the Moderns.*

THIS little Tract I have introduced with a short General View *of the whole* System *of* Learning, *wherein young Students may at once behold, as it were in Miniature, the Objects, Boundaries, Ends and Uses of each of the Sciences; their Foundation in the Nature of Things; the natural Order wherein they lie, and their several Relations and Connections, both with Respect to one another, and to the general End, viz.* our Happiness, *pursued thro' them all.*

THIS seems to me as useful in the Instruction of young Beginners in the Sciences, as it is in teaching Geography *to exhibit, first of all, a general Map of the whole terraqueous Globe, in order to a more particular Description of the several Countries and Kingdoms in the following Maps; or in teaching* Astronomy, *to give first a general Delineation of the whole System of the World, in order to account for the* Phænomena *in the several particular Planets in the following Schemes. For, as in the* natural World, *one cannot have a just Notion of any particular Country, without considering its Situation in relation to the whole Globe, nor of any particular Globe, without considering its Situation with respect to the whole System; so in the* intellectual World *(if I may so call it) neither can one have a just Notion of any particular Science, without considering it as it stands related to the whole* Circle of Learning, *and the general End pursued through the Whole. And such a short Draught may also be of some Use to Students, to direct and methodize their Thoughts, and enlarge their Minds, and at the same time engage their Application and Industry in the Pursuit of their Studies.*

AN

ERRATA:

Which the Reader is desired to correct with his Pen, before he proceeds to read these Tracts.

In the NOETICA.

PAGE ix. *read*, LEARNING (which the *Grecians* called *Cyclopædia)* implies, *&c.*

Page 17. *for* ΩN, *read*, ON, and ὁ οντως ων.

Page 24. Line *ult.* for *ſina*, read *ſine*.

Page 30. l. 24, *read*, on *Account of* which

Page 36. l. 3, put a (,) after is,---and l. 13, *read*, as a Subſtance.

Page 40. l. 17, *for* Ideas, *read* Idea.

Page 62. l. 19, put (;) after univerſal ;----and l. 21. put (:) after Affirmative :

Page 77. Margin, *read*, *learning Connexions*, without the (,)

Page 87. l. 4, *read* Globes, a conſiderable Notion, *&c.*

Page 90. l. 9, *after* Elaſticity, *inſert* Electricity ;---and l. 17, *read* Contrivance.

In the ETHICA.

Title Page, for *noctis*, read *noctes*.

Page 3. l. 19, *read*, of a rational, *&c.*

Page 6. in the Margin, read *Hutcheſon*.

Page 8. l. 28, *for* enjoying, *read* enjoining.

Page 9. l. 9. *read*, many other Laws may be added, *&c.*

Page 11. l. 30, for *Who*, read *What am I?*

Page 17. l. 7, *for* cannot, *read* can, not only, *&c.*

Page 25. l. 24, *read* Τȣ γαρ και γενος, *&c.*

Page 57. l. 15, *after* Him, *inſert* (P. I. Ch. II. § 19.)

Page 68. l. 7, *read*, of my Exiſtence, *&c.*

Page 88. l. 20, *read*, there is, on the Side of Virtue, the trueſt, *&c.*

Page 95. l. 19, *read*, had ever been known before.

AN INTRODUCTION TO THE STUDY of PHILOSOPHY.

Exhibiting a general View of all the Parts of LEARNING.

Quod si cuique scientiæ provincia sua tribuatur, limites assignentur, principia & objecta accurate distinguantur, quæ ad singulas pertinent, tractare licuerit, majore, tum facilitate, tum perspicuitate. D. BERK. DE MOT.

1. LEARNING implies the Knowledge of every Thing useful to our Well-being and true Happiness in this Life, or our supreme Happiness in the Life to come. And as our *Happiness* consists in the Enjoyment of *Truth* and *Good*, by the right Exercise of our Understandings, Affections, Wills and active Powers, it must take in every Thing that relates both to *Theory* and *Practice*, *i. e.* both to *Science* and *Art*; for *Science* is the Knowledge of Truth considered speculatively, and *Art* is the Knowledge of Truth considered as directive of our Practice for the attaining our true Good or Happiness. And all the various

Parts of Learning may be reduced to theſe two; *Philology*, or the Study of *Words* and other Signs, and *Philoſophy*, or the Study of the *Things* ſignified by them. And,

2. (I.) As the Underſtandings of young Perſons, for the firſt fifteen or ſixteen Years of their Life, are not ripe enough to enter into the ſublimer Studies of *Philoſophy*, it is neceſſary that during this Stage they ſhould be chiefly employ'd in the Study of *Philology*, or the Languages, to which ſhould be added the firſt Things in the *Mathematicks*, both which are moſt level to their juvenile Capacities, as they chiefly depend on the Imagination and Memory, which in Youth are moſt vigorous and tenacious.

3. (1.) WITH regard to Language, they muſt be early initiated in the Rudiments of *Grammar*, or the Rules of *Speech*, relating both to the Accidents and Connection of Words, and this both in their Mother Tongue, and other Languages, eſpecially the *French*, *Latin*, *Greek* and *Hebrew*, in which let them go as far as may be in this firſt Stage of Life.

4. (2.) As ſoon as they have got a good Notion of *pure Speech* by the Study of *Grammar*, let them learn the Nature of *figurative Speech* in *Rhetorick:* And from thence, as they go on to read the Claſſicks, let them learn the Uſe of the various Tropes and Figures in *Oratory*, which is the Art of true Eloquence, and explains the Topicks of Invention, the Rules of Diſpoſition or Order, and of Elocution or Delivery. And,

5. (3.) As they go on to read the ancient Hiſtorians, let them apply themſelves to the Study of *Hiſtory*, conſidered as the Art of an elegant and juſt Narration of true Matters of Fact for

for the Benefit of Poſterity. And that they may underſtand the Ancients the better, they ſhould read the beſt modern Writers of Hiſtory, which that they may read with Advantage, they ought to have ſome eaſy Inſtruction in *Geography* and *Chronology*, and make uſe of the beſt ancient and modern Maps of thoſe Places, and Tables of thoſe Times, to which their Books relate, which will render what they read the more intelligible, and take the deeper Impreſſion on their Memories. * "History is a large Field, in which they will ſee the wonderful Series of Providence; ſtrange Turns of Fortune, ſurprizing Occurrences, and an amazing Variety of Accidents; fooliſh Mortals labouring for Trifles, contending eagerly for Things they would be much happier without; ſome curſed in having their Wiſhes, raiſed to the utmoſt Height of Power and Grandeur, only to be thrown down thence with the greater Obloquy and Contempt; others pleaſing themſelves with their Obſcurity, and laughing at the Noiſe and Buſtle that ſurrounds them." All which tend to give the Youth a good Inſight into human Nature, and lead them to true Wiſdom in their own Conduct.

6. (4.) As they go on to read the Poets, they ſhould get ſome Knowledge of *Poetry*, conſidered as an Art, being a juſt and lively Deſcription of Things or Perſons, either real or imaginary, with an Elevation and Dignity of Thought, and with the Advantages of Numbers and Harmony, and every Kind of Ornament that Language is capable of, which will qualify them the better to entertain themſelves with thoſe great Maſters of Wit and Eloquence. "There is ſomething charming

* *Vide* Magazine for *October*, 1748.

charming in Verſe; ſomething that ſtrikes the Ear, moves the Soul, rouſes the Paſſions, and engages the Affections," while it fills the Soul with the moſt uſeful Inſtructions, attended with the moſt exquiſite Delight. "It ſeems to have been the firſt Way of Writing, and in ſome Countries even older than Letters, and conſequently to have been the Voice of infant Nature in her early Bloom and native Sweetneſs. In it the Ancients explained their Sentiments, conveyed their Laws, and delivered their Precepts of Morality in Fable; the People liked the Inſtructions which came to them attended with Delight; and as they heard them with Pleaſure, ſo they retained them with Eaſe." To this Head of Language belongs the *Art of Criticiſm*, which teaches the true Force of Words and Phraſes, the Nature of Stile, and a true Taſte, ſo as to make a right Judgment of the Beauties and Excellencies of any Performance in either of theſe Kinds of Writings.

7. WHILE Youth are acquainting themſelves with the Rudiments of *Eloquence*, *Hiſtory* and *Poetry*, they ſhould alſo be learning the firſt and eaſieſt Things in the *Mathematicks* (which indeed, as well as Words, do in ſome Meaſure belong to the Doctrine of Signs) eſpecially Things that relate to Practice, both in *Arithmetick* and *Geometry*, which will very much tend to engage and ſtrengthen their Attention, enlarge their Capacities, and ripen their Minds. And ſomething of *natural Hiſtory*, with the Arts of *Drawing* and *Muſick*, if they have a Taſte for it, will be very pleaſant and uſeful Amuſements. And theſe Studies which they have begun in this firſt Period, and (it is to be hoped) made a conſiderable Progreſs

grefs in, muft be afterwards continued and carried to further Perfection, and made their Diverfion at Turns, while they

8. (II.) PROCEED, *fecondly*, to the further Improvement of their Underftandings and active Powers, in the fublimer Studies of *Philofophy*, which is the Study of Truth and Wifdom, or the Knowledge of *Things*, as being what they really are, together with a Conduct correfpondent thereunto, in the Purfuit of true Happinefs; to which they muft go on when they are fixteen or feventeen Years old, "And what concerns us in thefe more exalted Studies is, that we be very exact and careful to attend more to Things than Words, and endeavour to make fuch Things our own as will prove real Accomplifhments to our Minds, and duly regulate both our Tempers and Manners; and fuch are the Knowledge of GOD and *ourfelves*, for *Philofophia eft Rerum Divinarum Humanarumque Scientia*, as *Tully* defines it, and comprehendeth every Thing, both fpeculative and practical, upon thefe large and comprehenfive Subjects.

9. THE firft, which relates to GOD, takes in the whole Creation; the full Extent of Being; for by the Contemplation of the Effects we arife to the Caufe. "And as by confidering that wonderful and amazing Power, that All-comprehending Wifdom, that inimitable Beauty, that furprizing Harmony, that immutable Order, which abundantly difcover themfelves in the Formation and Government of the Univerfe, we are led to their divine Original, who is the inexhaufted Source, the glorious Fountain of all Perfection;" fo by making due Reflections on the Operations of our own Minds, and the large Ex-

tent of our intellectual Faculties and their Objects; their several distinct Exertions, and their Subserviency to each other; the free Activity of our Souls, and the various Passions that put them on Action for attaining our several Ends; and the various Ways wherein they exert themselves, and exercise their Dominion over our Bodies; we may attain, in some good Measure, the Knowledge of ourselves, as well as of GOD, our chief Good, and the certain Means we must use, and the Method we must take to secure our true Happiness in the Enjoyment of Him, ourselves, and one another. In order to the raising our Minds to these sublime Speculations, and to regulate our Actions in these noble Pursuits, it is necessary that we be able to form to ourselves clear Ideas and Conceptions of those *Beings* or Things on which we contemplate, whether *Bodies* or *Spirits*: To the Attainment of which,

10. (1.) *LOGICK*, or the Art of Reasoning, is very requisite, the Foundation of which is *Metaphysicks*, or the *Philosophia prima*, which, by some, hath been called *Ontology*, and is the noblest and most elevated Part of Science. It begins with sensible Objects, and from them takes its Rise to Things purely intellectual, and treats of *Being* abstracted from every particular Nature, whether *Body* or *Spirit*, and of all the general Distinctions, Connections and Relations of Things, whether sensible or intellectual, and so lays a Foundation for clear and just Reasoning, while we proceed upon stable and unerring Principles. Which Foundation being laid, *Logick* teacheth us the Rules of thinking regularly, and *reasoning* justly, whereby we learn to distinguish *Truth* from *Falshood*, and proceed from Things *simple* to Things *compound*,

compound, and from Things precarious and *contingent* to Things *neceſſary*, ſtable and eternal, which therefore will reſult in the cleareſt and juſteſt Views, both of all other Things, and of the adorable Excellencies of the divine Nature, that our little Minds are capable of.

11. (2.) FROM theſe general Principles and Laws of Reaſoning, we proceed to the Application of them, firſt in the Study of *Quantity* in general, whether *Number* or *Magnitude*, in the ſublimer *Mathematicks*, or the Arts of Computation. And here again opens a noble Scene of eternal Truth, in the Demonſtration of a vaſt Number of Theorems and Problems, both *Arithmetical* and *Geometrical*, to which *Algebra* is wonderfully ſubſervient, in the Contemplation both of *Lines*, *Surfaces* and *Solids*, in all their endleſs Varieties and Proportions; which will enable us to proceed with the greater Advantage in the Study of Nature, and without which we cannot read with Underſtanding the beſt Things that have been written on that Subject. This Sort of Study hath likewiſe a direct Tendency to lead us to an admiring Senſe of the Deity, in whoſe infinite Treaſures of eternal Truth, we behold theſe Connections and Demonſtrations, who hath made all Things in Number, Meaſure and Weight. To this Head belong, *Trigonometry*, *Geodæſia*, *Stereometry*, the Doctrine of the *Sphere* and *Cylinder*, and of *Conic Sections* and *Fluxions*.

12. (3.) FROM the Contemplation of Quantity in the *Abſtract*, we go on next to the Conſideration of it in *Concrete*, or in the Objects of Senſe, *i. e.* as blended with the other ſenſible Qualities, in the endleſly various Bodies that compoſe this mighty Frame of Heaven and

Earth, and the Principles and Laws of Motion, on which their Phænomena depend, which are the Subjects of *Physicks* or *natural Philosophy*: The Foundation of which is *Mechanicks*, which explain the Nature of *Bodies* in *general*, and the *Forces* by which they move; and demonstrate the various Laws of their *Motion*. To which belong *Staticks*, *Hydrostaticks* and *Pneumaticks*. Upon which we proceed in *Geology*, or *Physicks*, strictly so called, to contemplate this *Globe of Earth*, in all its Parts and Furniture; the Elements, Fire, Air, Water and Earth; the Stones, Mines, Minerals, Meteors, Plants, and Animals, and particularly the wonderful Structure of our own Bodies. Here therefore belong, *Opticks*, *Musick*, *Geography*, *Navigation* and *Commerce*; *Lithology*, *Metallology* and *Meteorology*, *Agriculture*, *Chemistry* and *Botanics*, *Anatomy*, *Surgery* and *Medicine*, and every Thing useful in Life. And, lastly, from the Earth we launch forth into the vast and unmeasurable Æther, and in *Astronomy* we contemplate the *Heavens* and *Stars*, both fixed and erratick; and particularly our *Sun*, with his splendid Chorus of *Planets* and *Comets*, with their Orbits, Magnitudes and Densities, and the Laws of their Motions in the Tides of their Fluids, and their diurnal and annual Revolutions: To which belong *Chronology* and *Dialling*. And the *Facts* in all *Nature* are related in *Natural History*. "All which open upon us an amazing Scene, in which Nature displays her surprizing *Phænomena*, and invites us heedfully to consider her wonderful Productions, and trace out infinite Wisdom, Power and Goodness, thro' the immense Spaces, from the Heights above to the Depths below, from the glorious

Orbs

Orbs which roll over our Heads, to the minuteſt Inſects that crawl under our Feet, and even Things either vaſtly minute or diſtant that eſcape the Ken of our naked Eye. From all which we are led to behold, acknowledge, admire and adore the great Author of all Things." And this prepares us,

13. (4.) To proceed a Step higher, and from the *Senſible* or *Natural World*, to go on to the Contemplation of the *Intelligent* or *Moral World*; from the World of *Bodies*, to the World of *Spirits*, which, as ſuch, being intelligent and moral Agents, are the great Subject of *Ethics*, or *moral Philoſophy*. The Foundation of which is *Pneumatology*, or the Doctrine of *Spirits*; in which, we begin with our own Souls, their Powers and Operations, both perceptive and active; and thence proceed to other Orders of Intelligences, and ſo gradually riſe to the more particular Contemplation of the DEITY, the great Father of Spirits, and the ſupreme Lord and Governor of the whole Creation, which is called *Theology*. And when we have learn'd juſt Notions of Him and ourſelves, we from thence demonſtratively deduce the great Principles of that Duty which we owe to Him, ourſelves and one another (which opens another glorious Scene of eternal Truth) the Performance of which, doth, in the Nature of it, tend to our higheſt Perfection and Happineſs. All which great Branches of Duty are the Subject of *Ethics* (ſtrictly ſo called) which is the Art of living happily by the univerſal Practice of Virtue. But theſe Things will be beſt learn'd from the *Sacred Volumes*, the Deſign and Buſineſs of which is to explain and inforce the great Principles of *Theology* and *Morality* by

Divine

Divine Revelation; particularly "our blessed Saviour hath exalted *Ethics* to the sublimest Pitch, and his admirable Sermon in the Mount is the noblest and exactest Model of Perfection."

14. (5.) *Ethics* explain the Laws of our Duty as we are Men in general, and which indeed are the eternal and immutable Laws of Right that equally bind all intelligent Creatures. But as we cannot well subsist without being combined into particular *Societies*: And as Societies are of two Kinds; the one founded in Nature, *viz. Families*, the other in Compact, *viz. Civil Governments*: Hence spring two other Branches of *Moral Philosophy*, viz. *Œconomics*, which relate to the Regulation of *Families*; and *Politicks*, which treat of the Constitution and good Government of *Cities*, *Kingdoms* and *Republicks*. And as good *Policy* provides for every Thing that may contribute to the publick Good and Happiness of Mankind, it does, in Effect, comprehend and sum up the whole of *Philosophy*. And, lastly, as it provides for the Happiness of Men, both *Temporal* and *Spiritual*, both with Regard to this Life, and that which is to come, it must consist of two great Branches, *viz. Civil* and *Ecclesiastical Polity*. And the Facts in the *Moral World* are related in *Biography*, and in *Civil* and *Ecclesiastical History*. The whole may be seen in one View in the following Table.

The

The TABLE.

LEARNING is the Knowledge of every Thing that may contribute to our true Happiness, both in Theory and Practice, and consists of two Parts.

- I. *Philology*, or the Study of Words and other Signs, & is,
  - 1. *General* or common to all Kinds of Speaking, in
    - 1. *Grammar*, of pure Language.
    - 2. *Rhetorick*, of figurative Speech.
  - 2. *Special*, or of particular Kinds of Speaking or Writing, as,
    - 1. *Oratory*, which treats of true Eloquence.
    - 2. *History*, which relates real Facts.
    - 3. *Poetry*, which describes Things, either real or imaginary. To all which belongs the *Art* of *Criticism*.
- II. *Philosophy*, or the Study of the Things signified by them, whether Bodies or Spirits, or any Thing relating to them, and is,
  - 1. *General* or common to all Kinds of Beings, and is,
    - 1. *Rational*, in *Metaphysicks* and *Logick*, which cultivate our rational Powers.
    - 2. *Mathematical*, which teach us to reason on abstract Quantity, Number and Magnitude, in *Arithmetick* and *Geometry*, the Arts of Numbering and Measuring.
  - 2. *Special*, or peculiar to each Kind of Beings, and is,
    - 1. *Natural*, which teacheth the Knowledge of the natural World, or of Bodies, in *Mechanicks*, *Physicks* and *Astronomy*, which explain the Phænomena both in Heaven and Earth.
    - 2. *Moral*, which teacheth the Knowledge of the moral World or Spirits, and is
      - 1. *Speculative* in *Pneumatology* and *Theology*, of Spiritual Beings, and especially GOD the Father of all.
      - 2 *Practical*, in 1. *Ethics*, of Behaviour in general. 2. *OEconomics*, of the Conduct of Families. And 3. *Politics*, of the Government of States, *Civil* and *Ecclesiastical*.

The

THE

CONTENTS

Of the following TRACT.

CHAP I.

Of the Mind in general, *its* Objects *and* Operations.

CHAP.

CHAP II.

Of the Mind simply apprehending, *and of* its Objects *more particularly.*

27. *Par-*

CHAP. III.

Of the Mind, judging, affirming, denying, assenting, &c.

CHAP. IV.

Of the Mind reasoning and methodizing its Thoughts.

CHAP. V.

Of the Mind, affecting, willing *and* acting.

CHAP. VI.

Of the Progress of the Mind, towards its highest Perfection.

NOETICA:

NOETICA:

OR

The first PRINCIPLES of METAPHYSICS *and* LOGIC.

Together with

The *Progress* of the *Human Mind* towards its *Perfection.*

CHAP. I.

Of the Mind in general, *its* Objects *and* Operations.

§ 1. IT is my Design in the following Essay, to trace out, in as short a Compass as I can, the several Steps of the Mind of Man, from the first Impressions of Sense, through the several Improvements it gradually makes, till it arrives to that Perfection and Enjoyment of itself, which is the great End of its Being.-----In order to which, it will first be expedient to define what we mean by the *Human Mind*, and to give some Account of its various Objects, Powers and Operations, and the Principles and Rules by which they are to be conducted in attaining to the Know-

The Design.

ledge of Truth, which is the Business of that Science which is called *LOGIC*, or *The Art of Thinking* or *Reasoning*; the Foundation of which is the *Philosophia prima*, which is also called *Metaphysics* and *Ontology*, or *the Doctrine of the general Notion of Being, with its various Properties and Affections*, and *those applied in general both to Body and Spirit*. And as *Truth* and *Good* are nearly allied, being in effect but the same Thing under different Considerations; this will pave the Way towards the Attainment of that supreme Good, in the Choice and Enjoyment of which consists our highest Happiness; the particular Consideration of which is the Business of *Ethics*, or *Moral Philosophy*, which is *the Art of pursuing our highest Happiness by the universal Practice of Virtue*.

The Definition of Mind.

§ 2. THE Word *Mind* or *Spirit*, in general, signifies any *intelligent active Being*; which Notion we take from what we are conscious of in ourselves, who know that we have within us a Principle of conscious Perception, Intelligence, Activity and Self-exertion; or rather, that each of us is a conscious, perceptive, intelligent, active and self-exerting Being: And by Reasoning and Analogy from ourselves we apply it to all other Minds or Intelligences besides, or superior to us; and (removing all Limitations and Imperfections) we apply it even to that *Great Supreme Intelligence*, who is the universal Parent of all created Spirits, and (as far as our Words and Conceptions can go) may be defined, *an infinite Mind* or *Spirit*, or *a Being infinitely intelligent and active*. But by the *Human Mind*, we mean that Principle of Sense, Intelligence and free Activity, which we feel within in ourſelves, or rather feel ourſelves to be, furniſhed with thoſe Objects and Powers, and under thoſe Confinements and Limitations, under which it hath pleaſed our great Creator to place us in this preſent State.

Of the Union of Body and Mind.

§ 3. We are, at preſent, *Spirits* or *Minds* connected with groſs, *tangible Bodies*, in ſuch a Manner, that as our Bodies, can perceive and act nothing but by our Minds, ſo, on the other Hand, our Minds perceive and act by Means of our bodily Organs. Such is the preſent Law of our Nature, which I conceive to be no other than a meer arbitrary Conſtitution or Eſtabliſhment of Him that hath made us to be what we are.---And accordingly I apprehend that the Union between our Souls and Bodies, during our preſent State, conſiſts in nothing elſe but this Law of our Nature, which is the Will and perpetual *Fiat* of that infinite Parent Mind, who made, and *holds our Souls in Life*, and *in whom we live, and move, and have our Being*, viz. That our Bodies ſhould be thus acted by our Minds, and that our Minds ſhould thus perceive and act by the Organs of our Bodies, and under ſuch Limitations as in fact we find ourſelves to be attended with.

Definition of Idea, Notion, &c.

§ 4. The immediate Object of theſe our Perceptions and Actions we call *Ideas*; as this Word has been commonly defined and uſed by the Moderns, with whom it ſignifies any immediate Object of the Mind in Thinking, whether ſenſible or intellectual, and ſo is, in Effect, ſynonymous with the Word *Thought*, which comprehends both.-----*Plato*, indeed, by the Word *Idea*, underſtood the original Exemplar of Things, whether ſenſible or intellectual, in the eternal Mind, conformable to which all Things exiſt; or the abſtract Eſſences of Things, as being Originals or *Archetypes* in that infinite Intellect, of which our Ideas or Conceptions are a Kind of Copies.----But perhaps, for the more diſtinct underſtanding ourſelves upon this Subject, it may be beſt to confine the Word *Idea* to the immediate Objects of Senſe and Imagination, which was the original Meaning of it; and to uſe the Word *Notion* or *Conception*, to ſignify the Objects of Conſciouſneſs and pure Intellect, tho' both of them may be expreſſed by the general Term *Thought*; for theſe are ſo entirely, and *toto Cælo* different and diſtinct one from the other, that it may be apt to breed Confuſion in our Thoughts and Language, to uſe the ſame Word promiſcuouſly for them both; tho' we are indeed generally obliged to ſubſtitute ſenſible Images and the Words annexed to them, to repreſent Things purely intellectual; ſuch, for Inſtance, are the Words, *Spirit*, *Reflect*, *Conceive*, *Diſcourſe*, and the like.

The Original of our Ideas.

§ 5. OUR Minds may be ſaid to be created meer *Tabulæ raſæ*; i. e. They have no Notices of any Objects of any Kind properly created in them, or concreated with them: Yet I apprehend, that in all the Notices they have of any Kind of Objects, they have an immediate Dependance upon the Deity, as really as they depend upon Him for their Exiſtence; *i. e.* They are no more Authors to themſelves of the Objects of their Perceptions, or the Light by which they perceive them, than of the Power of Perceiving itſelf; but that they perceive them by a perpetual Inter-

courſe

course with that great Parent Mind, to whose incessant Agency they are entirely passive, both in all the Perceptions of Sense, and in all that intellectual Light by which they perceive the Objects of the pure Intellect.-------Notwithstanding which, it is plain from Experience, that in Consequence of these Perceptions they are entirely at Liberty to act, or not to act, and all their Actions flow from a Principle of Self-exertion.-----But in order the better to understand these Things, I must more particularly define these Terms.----And, as all the Notices we have in our Minds derive to them originally from (or rather by Means of) these two Fountains, *Sense* and *Consciousness*, it is necessary to begin with them.

Of the Senses;

§ 6. By *Sense*, we mean, those Perceptions we have of Objects *ab extra*, or by Means of the several Organs of our Bodies.---Thus, by *Feeling* or Touch, we perceive an endless Variety of *tangible Objects*, *Resistance*, *Extension*, *Figure*, *Motion*, *Hard*, *Soft*, *Heat*, *Cold*, &c. By *Sight* we perceive *Light* and *Colours*, with all their endlesly various Modifications, *Red*, *Blue*, *Green*, &c.---By *Hearing*, we perceive *Sounds* :---By *Tasting*, *Sapors* :---By *Smelling*, *Odours*, &c.---These are called *Simple Ideas*.---And of these, sorted out into a vast Variety of fixed Combinations, or *Compound Ideas*, distinct from each other, and in which they are always found to co-exist, consists every Sort and individual *Body* in Nature, such as we call *Man*, *Horse*, *Tree*, *Stone*, *Apple*, *Cherry*, &c.-----And of all these various distinct Combinations or Compounds, connected together in such a Manner as to constitute one most beautiful, useful and harmonious Whole, consists what we call *Universal Nature*, or the intire *sensible* or *natural World*.

 § 7. In

§ 7. In the Perception of these Ideas or Objects of Sense, we find our Minds are meerly passive, it not being in our Power (supposing our Organs rightly disposed and situated) whether we will see Light and Colours, hear Sounds, &c. We are not Causes to ourselves of these Perceptions, nor can they be produced in our Minds without a Cause; or (which is the same Thing) by any imagined unintelligent, inert, or unactive Cause (which indeed is a Contradiction in Terms) from whence it is Demonstration that they must derive to us from an Almighty, intelligent active Cause, exhibiting them to us, impressing our Minds with them, or producing them in us; and consequently (as I intimated) it must be by a perpetual Intercourse of our Minds with the DEITY, the great Author of our Beings, or by His perpetual Influence or Activity upon them, that they are possessed of all these Objects of Sense, and the Light by which we perceive them.

In which we are passive.

§ 8. These Ideas or Objects of Sense are commonly supposed to be Pictures or Representations of Things without us, and indeed external to any Mind, even that of the Deity himself, and the Truth or Reality of them is conceived to consist in their being exact Pictures of Things or Objects without us, which are supposed to be the real Things.---But as it is impossible for us to know what is without our Minds, and consequently, what those supposed Originals are, and whether these Ideas of ours are just Resemblances of them or not; I am afraid this Notion of them will lead us into an inextricable Scepticism. I am therefore apt to think that these

Ideas of Sense not Pictures, but the real Things.

these Ideas, or immediate Objects of Senſe, are the real Things, at leaſt all that we are concerned with, I mean, of the ſenſible Kind; and that the Reality of them conſiſts in their Stability and Conſiſtence, or their being, in a ſtable Manner, exhibited to our Minds, or produced in them, and in a ſteady Connection with each other, conformable to certain fixed Laws of Nature, which the great *Father of Spirits* hath eſtabliſhed to Himſelf, according to which He conſtantly operates and affects our Minds, and from which He will not vary, unleſs upon extraordinary Occaſions, as in the Caſe of Miracles.

Inſtanced in Things viſible and tangible.

§ 9. THUS, for Inſtance, there is a fixed ſtable Connection between *Things tangible* and *Things viſible*, or the immediate Objects of *Touch* and *Sight*, depending, as I conceive, immediately upon the permanent, moſt wiſe and Almighty Will and *Fiat* of the great Creator and Preſerver of the World. By which, neither can it be meant, that viſible Objects are Pictures of tangible Objects (which yet is all the Senſe that can be made of our Ideas of Senſe being Images of real Things without us) for they are entirely different and diſtinct Things; as different as the ſound *Triangle*, and the Figure ſignified by it; ſo different, that a Man born blind, and made to ſee, could have no more Notion that a viſible Globe hath any Connection with a tangible Globe, by meer Sight, without being taught, than a *Frenchman* that ſhould come into *England*, and hear the Word *Man*, could imagine, without being taught, that it ſignified the ſame Thing with the Word *Homme*, in his Language.---All that can be meant by it, therefore, is, That, as *tangible Things* are the Things immediately capable of producing (or rather, being attended with) ſenſible Pleaſure or Pain in us, according to the preſent Laws of our Nature, on Account of which they are conceived of as being properly the *real Things*; ſo the immediate *Objects of Sight* or *viſible Things*, are always, by the ſame ſtable Law of our Nature, connected with them, as Signs of them, and ever correſpondent and proportioned to them; *Viſible Extenſion*, *Figure*, *Motion*, &c. with thoſe of the *tangible Kind*, which go by the ſame Names; and ſo in the Compounds or Combinations of them; the viſible *Man*, *Horſe*, *Tree*, *Stone*, &c. with thoſe of the tangible Kind, ſignified by the ſame Names.*

Of Archetypes.

§ 10. NOT that it is to be doubted but that there are *Archetypes* of theſe ſenſible Ideas exiſting, external to our Minds; but then they muſt exiſt in ſome other Mind, and be Ideas alſo as well as ours; becauſe an Idea can reſemble nothing but an Idea; and an Idea ever implies in the very Nature of it, Relation to a Mind perceiving it, or in which it exiſts. But then thoſe Archetypes or Originals, and the Manner of their Exiſtence in that eternal Mind, muſt be intirely different from that of their Exiſtence in our Minds; as different, as the Manner of His Exiſtence is from that of ours: In Him they muſt exiſt, as in original Intellect; in us, only by Way of Senſe and Imagination; and in Him, as Originals; in us, only as faint Copies; ſuch as he thinks fit to communicate to us, according to ſuch Laws and Limitations as he hath eſtabliſhed, and ſuch as are ſufficient to all the Purpoſes

* See Bp. *Berkeley's Theories of Viſion, Principles of Human Knowledge*, and *Three Dialogues*.

Purposes relating to our Well-being, in which only we are concerned. Our Ideas, therefore, can no otherwise be said to be Images or Copies of the Archetypes in the eternal Mind, than as our Souls are said to be Images of Him, or as we are said to be *made after his Image.**

§ 11. THUS much for *Sense.*---By *Consciousness* is meant, our Perception of Objects *ab intra*, or from reflecting or turning the Eye of our Mind inward, and observing what passeth within itself; whereby we know that we perceive all those sensible Objects and their Connections, and all the Pleasures and Pains attending them, and all the Powers or Faculties of our Minds employed about them. Thus I am conscious that I perceive *Light* and *Colours*, *Sounds*, *Odours*, *Sapors*, and *tangible Qualities*, with all the various Combinations of them; and that of these, some give me, or rather are attended with *Pain* or Uneasiness, others with *Pleasure* or Ease, and the comfortable Enjoyment of myself. I find, moreover, that when I have had any Perception or Impression of Sense, I retain a faint *Image* of it in my Mind afterwards, or have a Kind of internal Sense or Remembrance of it; as having seen the *Sun*, a *Flower*, a *Horse*, or a *Man*, I retain the Image of their Figure, Shape, Colour, &c. afterwards. Thus I have now a faint Idea of the *Sun* at Midnight, and of a *Rose* in Winter: I know how such a *Tree*, such a *Horse*, or such a *Man* looks, tho' I have neither of them before my Eyes. This Power of the Mind is called *Imagination* and *Memory*, which implies a Consciousness of the original Impression (tho' indeed the

Of Consciousness, Imagination and Memory.

* See on this Head, *Norris's Ideal World.* Part 1.

the Word *Memory* may imply the Recollection of intellectual as well as ſenſible Objects, but chiefly thoſe by Means of theſe, which is alſo called *Reminiſcence)* and theſe Ideas of the Imagination may be truly ſaid to be Images or Pictures of the Ideas or immediate Objects of Senſe. We are moreover conſcious of a Power whereby we can, not only imagine Things as being what they really are in Nature, but can alſo join ſuch Parts and Properties of Things together, as never co-exiſted in Nature, but are meer Creatures of our Minds, or Chimeras; as the Head of a Man with the Body of an Horſe, *&c.* which muſt alſo be referred to the Imagination, but as influenced by the Will.

Of the pure Intellect, and its Acts.

§ 12. BUT beſides theſe Powers of *Senſe* and *Imagination*, we are conſcious of what is called the *pure Intellect*, or the Power of conceiving of abſtracted or *ſpiritual Objects*, and the *Relations* between our ſeveral Ideas and Conceptions, and the various Diſpoſitions, Exertions and Actions of our Minds, and the complex Notions reſulting from all theſe; of all which we cannot be properly ſaid to have *Ideas*, they being intirely of a different Kind from the Objects of Senſe and Imagination, on which Account I would rather call them *Notions* or *Conceptions*. And they are either *ſimple*, ſuch as *Perception*, *Conſciouſneſs*, *Volition*, *Affection*, *Action*, &c. or *complex*, as *Spirit*, *Soul*, *God*, *Cauſe*, *Effect*, *Proportion*, *Juſtice*, *Charity*, &c. And of all theſe, and what relates to them, conſiſts the intire *ſpiritual* or *moral World*. But in order the better to underſtand or conceive of theſe, it is neceſſary more particularly to purſue and explain theſe intellectual and active

active Powers, whereof we are conscious within ourselves; such as, 1. The *simple Apprehension* of Objects, and their several Relations, Conections and Dependencies, arising from our comparing our Ideas and Conceptions one with another. 2. *Judging* of *true* or *false*, according as Things appear to agree or disagree, to be connected or not connected one with another; and 3. *Reasoning* or inferring one Thing from another, and methodizing them according to their Connections and Order: All which are the Subject of *Logics.* To which succeed, 1. *Affecting* or *Disaffecting* them according as they appear *good* or *bad*, agreeable or disagreeable to us, *i. e.* attended with Pleasure or Uneasiness. 2. *Willing* or *Nilling*, *Chusing* or *Refusing* according as we affect or disaffect them. 3. *Liberty* of *Acting*, or forbearing to act in Consequence of the Judgment and Choice we have made of them: All which are the Subject of *Ethics.* It is necessary to define all these Terms, and give some Account of these several Acts and Exertions of our Minds (which, as well as those of Sense, Consciousness, Imagination and Memory above-mentioned, are only so many Modifications of them) in order to what is next to follow.

Of intellectual Light or intuitive Evidence.

§ 13. But before I proceed, I would, in order thereunto, first observe, That no sooner does any Object strike the Senses, or is received in our Imagination, or apprehended by our Understanding, but we are immediately conscious of a Kind of *intellectual Light* within us (if I may so call it) whereby we not only know that we perceive the Object, but directly apply ourselves to the Consideration of it, both in itself, its Properties

perties and Powers, and as it ſtands related to all other Things. And we find that as we are enabled by this *intellectual Light* to perceive theſe Objects and their various Relations, in like Manner as by *ſenſible Light* we are enabled to perceive the Objects of Senſe and their various Situations;* ſo our Minds are as paſſive to this *intellectual Light*, as they are to *ſenſible Light*, and can no more withſtand the Evidence of it, than they can withſtand the Evidence of Senſe. Thus I am under the ſame Neceſſity to aſſent to this, That *I am* or have a Being, and that I *perceive* and *freely exert myſelf*, as I am of aſſenting to this, That I *ſee Colours* or *hear Sounds*. I am as perfectly ſure that 2+2=4, or that the *Whole is equal to all its Parts*, as that I *feel Heat* or *Cold*, or that I *ſee the Sun* when I look full on it in the Meridian in a clear Day; *i. e.* I am intuitively certain of both.---This intellectual Light I conceive of as it were a *Medium* of Knowledge, as ſenſible Light is of Sight:------In both there is the *Power* of perceiving, and the *Object* perceived; and this is the *Medium* by which I am enabled to know it.---And this *Light* is one, and common to all intelligent Beings, and *enlighteneth* alike, *every Man that cometh into the World*, a *Chineſe*, or *Japoneſe*, as well as an *European* or *American*, and an *Angel* as well as a *Man*: By which they all at once ſee the ſame Thing to be true or right in all Places at the ſame Time, and alike invariably in all Times, paſt, preſent, and to come.

§ 14. Now if it be aſked, Whence does this Light derive, whereby all created Minds at once perceive, as by a common Standard, the ſame Things

* This is *Plato's* Doctrine, in his *Epinomis*, &c.

Things alike to be true and right?-----I anſwer, I have no other Way to conceive how I come to be affected with this intuitive intellectual Light, whereof I am conſcious, than by deriving it from the univerſal Preſence and Action of the DEITY, or a perpetual Communication with the great *Father of Lights*, * or rather his eternal *Word* and *Spirit*.---For I know I am not the Author of it to myſelf, being paſſive and not active with regard to it, tho' I am active in Conſequence of it.----Therefore, tho' I cannot explain the Manner how I am impreſſed with it (as neither can I that of Senſe) I do humbly conceive that God does as truly and immediately enlighten my Mind internally to know theſe intellectual Objects, as he does by the Light of the *Sun* (his ſenſible Repreſentative) enable me to perceive ſenſible Objects. So that thoſe Expreſſions are indeed no leſs Philoſophical than Devout, that GOD *is Light, and in his Light we ſee Light*.----And this intuitive Knowledge, as far as it goes, muſt be the *firſt Principles*, from which the Mind takes its Riſe, and upon which it proceeds in all its ſubſequent Improvements in Reaſoning, and diſcovering both Truth in Speculation, and Right in Action; ſo that this intellectual Light muſt be primarily and carefully attended to, if we would avoid and be ſecure from either Error or Vice.-----Nor muſt this Manner of Thinking be ſuſpected to favour of *Enthuſiaſm*, it being the ſettled Courſe or Law of Nature, according to which the great Parent Mind enlighteneth us; and that in Things, in their

Whence it is derived.

* See the *Archbiſhop* of *Cambray*, on this Subject, in his Demonſtration of the Exiſtence of God. And *Norris* or *Malbranch*.

their own Nature capable of clear Evidence; whereas *Enthusiasm* implies an *imaginary*, as *Revelation* is a real and well-attested adventitious Light, above and beyond the settled Law or Course of Nature, discovering Truths not otherwise knowable, and giving Directions, or enjoining Rules of Action in Things arbitrary, or Matters of meer Institution.---And from this intuitive intellectual Light it is (as I conceive) that we derive what we call *Taste* and *Judgment*, and, with respect to Morals, what some call the moral Sense or the Conscience, which are only a Sort of quick intuitive Sense or Apprehension of the Decent and Amiable, of Beauty and Deformity, of True and False, and of Right and Wrong, or Duty and Sin: And it is the chief Business of Culture, Art and Instruction, to awaken and turn our Attention to it, and assist us in making Deductions from it.

CHAP. II.

Of the Mind simply apprehending, *and of* its Objects *more particularly*.

§ 1. LET us therefore proceed to define the several Acts and Objects of the *pure Intellect* thus enlightened: And first, Of the *simple Apprehension* of Objects or *Beings*, and the various Conceptions arising to our View from the Consideration of their *Natures* and *Affections*, and their several *Relations*, Connections and Dependencies, such as *Cause* and *Effect*, *Essence* and *Existence*, Things *necessary* and *contingent*, *Finite* and

Of simple Apprehension and its Objects.

and *Infinite*, *Possible* and *Impossible*, *Perfect* and *Imperfect*, *Truth* and *Good*, *Beauty* and *Harmony*, *Substances* and *Accidents*, *Subjects* and *Adjuncts*, *Time* and *Place*, *Whole* and *Parts*, *Unity* and *Multiplicity*, *Number* and *Order*, *Identity* and *Diversity*, Things *Agreeing* and *Opposite*, *Equal* and *Unequal*, *Like* and *Unlike*, *Denomination* and *Definition*, *Individuals* and *Abstraction*, *Kinds* and *Sorts*, *Bodies* and *Spirits*; and lastly, of *Metaphor* and *Analogy* from Things sensible to Things spiritual, and from Things human to Things divine.---Of all which I shall treat in the Order as they are here enumerated.

Of Being in general.

§ 2. As soon as the Mind is possessed of any Variety of Objects, being assisted with that inward intellectual Light above-mentioned, deriving, and, as it were, perpetually beaming forth from the great Fountain of all Light, both sensible and intellectual, it immediately falls to contemplating its Ideas and Conceptions, and comparing them one with another.-----And here, the first Thing it is enlightened to know or be conscious of, is, its own Existence from the Existence of its Perceptions and Exertions and their Objects, which it conceives of as real *Beings* or *Things*, whence it gets the Notion of *Being* in general.---But even this first Object of its Knowledge it is made to know from that first Principle of intellectual Light, flowing from the Parent Mind, *That Perception and Action, and being perceived or acted upon, implies Existence*, of which Principle it has an inward intuitive Sense and Certainty. Hence it immediately infers, *I perceive and act, therefore I am: I perceive such an Object, therefore it is*, &c. Not that its Existence depends on my Mind, but on that Mind by by whom I am enabled to perceive it. And as perceiving and acting, and being perceived and acted upon, implies Exiſtence or *Being*, ſo it *is a Contradiction for the ſame Thing to be and not to be at the ſame Time*, for that would be to perceive and not perceive, to act and not to act, and to be perceived and not perceived, and acted upon and not acted upon, at one and the ſame Time : And from theſe Definitions ariſe that firſt great Diſtinction of *Being* into *Spirit* and *Body*, whereof the Exiſtence of the firſt conſiſts in perceiving and acting, and that of the other in being paſſively perceived and acted.---And here, to perceive or to act is called the *Power*, and what is perceived or acted upon, is called the *Object*.---So that by *Being*, is meant, what really IS or exiſts, in Oppoſition to what is merely fictitious or imaginary; a Creature of our own Minds, and not of him that made and enables us to perceive and act.

Of the firſt Being and eternal Truth.

§ 3. Now of every Thing that *IS*, it muſt be ſaid, either, That it *always was*; or, that it *began to be*.---If it always was, or never derived from the Power of any other Being, it muſt be independent of every other Being whatſoever, and conſequently muſt exiſt abſolutely by the intrinſic Neceſſity of its own Nature, or be a neceſſarily exiſtent Being, and all other Beings muſt depend on its Will and Power, otherwiſe they could never have been, or continue to be; and Itſelf, being derived from no other Being, and dependent on none, it muſt be out of the Power of any other Being to limit or controul it, and conſequently it muſt be *infinite* and *eternal*; *i. e.* muſt have all Reality, Perfection and Full-

Fulneſs of Being, without any regard to Time or Place: For that muſt be *infinite*, that has, and can have no poſſible Bounds or Limitations; and that muſt be *eternal*, that is, and always was, and will be, and can't but be; and ſuch a Being muſt be *All in All*; all Reality and Excellency.----Nor can there be more than *One* ſuch Being, who is *Being* itſelf, becauſe it is a manifeſt Contradiction that two or more Beings ſhould, each have in it, or conſiſt of, all poſſible Reality and Perfection. He muſt therefore be a perfect *Unity*, the TO E'N, and the TO 'ON, and the 'Οντως ὢν, as the Ancients called Him, which is the true Import of the original ſacred Names *JAH* and *JEHOVAH*. And He is alſo called *Truth* and *Good*:---*Truth* itſelf, as He is all Reality; and *Good* itſelf, as He is all Perfection and Excellency.---And He is *Truth* as He is infinitely intelligible, and *Good* as He is infinitely eligible, containing within and of Himſelf, all that can contribute to render Himſelf happy, as well as all other perceptive, conſcious, active Beings, dependent on Him.---In this neceſſarily exiſtent and eternal Being or Mind muſt originally exiſt all thoſe neceſſary and eternal Truths with which our Minds are furniſhed, either by Intuition or Demonſtration; ſuch as theſe, That *Perception and Action imply Exiſtence*:---That *what begins to be, muſt have a Cauſe*:---That *the Whole is equal to all its Parts*:---That *all the Rays of a Circle are equal*:---That *what is right or wrong in another towards me, muſt be equally right or wrong in me towards him*, &c.----We know that theſe and the like eternal Truths do not depend on our Minds, or the actual Exiſtence of Things, but muſt have an eternal and neceſſary Exiſtence, antecedent to our Knowledge of them,

 and

and independent of it, or of any particular Exiſtence.---And as we can have no Notion of Truth without a Mind perceiving it, their neceſſary and eternal Exiſtence muſt infer the neceſſary Exiſtence of an eternal Mind; and conſequently, it muſt be in that eternal Mind that we behold them, or rather by our Communication with Him that we are enlightened with the Knowledge of them.--- In Him they muſt exiſt as one archetypal and eternal Light of Truth; but as they are from Him reflected on the various Objects in our finite Minds, they appear various and manifold, as ſenſible Light is one in the Sun, tho' it becomes various Colours and other ſenſible Qualities in different Objects.

Of Cauſes & Effects.

§ 4. On the contrary, Whatever Being *began to be*, muſt have had a *Cauſe*, and depend on ſome other Being for its Exiſtence.----By the Word *Cauſe*, we mean, that Being by whoſe Deſign and Activity, Force or Exertion, another Being exiſts: And that Being which exiſts by the Deſign, Force, Action, or Exertion of another, is called an *Effect*; what is called an Effect therefore muſt be ſuppoſed not to have exiſted, and conſequently to have had a Beginning of Exiſtence, or at leaſt a dependent Exiſtence, and muſt therefore have had a Cauſe, by the Force or Activity of which it came into Exiſtence, and without which it would not have been.---And this muſt be the Caſe of every Thing that is, till you come to a *firſt Cauſe*, *i. e.* to a Being that never had a Beginning, or any dependent Exiſtence, but exiſts by the abſolute Neceſſity of its own Nature, having an original perfect Fulneſs of Being in and of itſelf, without depending on any other Being, and deals out Being and Perfection to all other

other Beings, in various Meaſures and Degrees as pleaſeth him.---And ſuch a Being there muſt be, otherwiſe nothing could ever have been, unleſs you ſuppoſe a Thing to be its own Cauſe, *i. e. To act before it is, which is impoſſible*; or unleſs you ſuppoſe an infinite Succeſſion of Cauſes and Effects, which in effect would be an infinite Effect without any Cauſe at all: * But *an Effect without a Cauſe, is a Contradiction in Terms*; for, by the Definition, to every Thing that is produced, there muſt be a correſpondent Power adequate to the Production of it, or an active Force ſufficient to produce it.---And here, the Thing exiſting is ſaid to be a Thing *in Act*; and as the Force producing adequate to the Effect, is called the Power, ſo the Effect not yet produced, is ſaid to be in Power, or *in fieri*, and the Being which exerts that Power, we call an *Agent* and *Active*, and that on or in which the Force terminates, we call a *Patient* and *Paſſive*.

Of real and apparent Cauſes.

§ 5. THERE are indeed many Things that occur to our Senſes and Thoughts, that appear at firſt Sight to be Agents or Cauſes, which, ſtrictly ſpeaking, are not ſo, as we find upon a more exact Scrutiny, though they are vulgarly ſo called. Thus we ſay, *The Sun moves, riſes and ſets*, when yet upon a more thorough Enquiry, we find, it is not the Action of the Sun, but theſe Appearances are occaſioned by the Motion of the Earth, and that they are only meer paſſive Appearances in our Minds. So we ſay, the *Fire burns*; the *Sun warms, enlivens, ripens the Fruits*, &c. and we call *the Parent the Cauſe of his Offspring*; whereas, upon a more ſtrict Enquiry, we find that he is by no Means the adequate Cauſe; and that the

 Sun,

* See *Wollaſton's Rel. of Nat.* p. 65, &c.

Sun, and (what we call) other natural Cauſes, are in themſelves but meer paſſive inert Beings, connected one with another, according to the eſtabliſhed Laws of Nature; ſo that being Things meerly paſſive and inert, they cannot, properly ſpeaking, be the Cauſes of the Effects vulgarly aſcribed to them; they muſt therefore be called only *Signs*, *Occaſions*, *Means*, or *Inſtruments*, and we muſt look for ſome other Being in whom reſides, and by whom muſt be exerted, that adequate Power or Force by which the Effect is truly produced, which therefore is the true and *real Cauſe*; and the other can only be called the *apparent* Cauſes, having no real Efficiency or Activity in the Production of the Effect.

Of neceſſary and voluntary Cauſes.

§ 6. MOREOVER we find from what we experience in ourſelves, that we breathe and our Blood circulates without any Deſign or Activity of ours; and the Courſe of Nature without us, goes on whether we will or not, and even tho' we ſhould exert our utmoſt Force to withſtand it. Theſe, with regard to us, may be called *neceſſary Effects*, as not depending on our Will and Power; tho' with regard to the true Author of Nature, they are free and *voluntary Effects.*---On the other Hand, we walk, ſpeak, write, *&c.* from a Principle of conſcious deſigned Self-exertion, and voluntary Activity; theſe therefore are called free or voluntary Effects with regard to us, which we produce or not, as we pleaſe; in doing which we are voluntary Cauſes. Hence we learn to make the Diſtinction between *neceſſary* and *voluntary*, or *free Cauſes* and *Effects.* So that by voluntary Effects, we mean, ſuch as are produced by a free voluntary Cauſe acting from

from a Principle of conſcious Deſign and Self-exertion, exciting a Force of its own, or from within itſelf, which it chuſeth to exert, and might do otherwiſe; and this is properly called a *Cauſe*, an efficient Cauſe or *Agent*. And as to thoſe *natural Effects* abovementioned, of which the apparent is not the real Cauſe, having neither Deſign nor Force in itſelf (as the Water in turning a Mill) but is rather acted than acts; however neceſſary they are with regard to us, yet from the moſt wiſe Deſign and Contrivance manifeſtly appearing in the Effects themſelves, we evidently diſcern that the Being who is their true and adequate Cauſe, muſt be furniſhed with Wiſdom and Power equal or ſufficient for the Production of them, and muſt act from a Principle of free Self-exertion, and with a Deſign or View at ſome certain End propoſed to himſelf in acting, and therefore be a free intelligent and *voluntary* Cauſe, for *nothing can give what it hath not.*

Of final Cauſes.

§ 7. WHENCE it appears, that only *intelligent active* Beings or Spirits, can be truly *efficient Cauſes*, which alone are properly called *Cauſes*, and that when we ſpeak of *natural Cauſes*, it is only in Accommodation to vulgar Apprehenſions, ſince they are meerly paſſive, and act, or rather are acted, without any Deſign or Exertion of their own.----And as to what are commonly called *final Cauſes*, they are only the Views or Motives, determining the Deſign or Purpoſe of the efficient Cauſe, but have properly no Cauſality or Activity in themſelves. We are conſcious, when we produce any Effect, that we act with ſome End, View, or Deſign, which determineth us, or rather, properly ſpeaking, upon the View of which we determine our-

 ſelves,

ſelves, to act ſo rather than otherwiſe, and to chuſe and make uſe of ſuch and ſuch Means, rather than others, as being moſt fit and uſeful in order to accompliſh our End; and therefore we ſay, *He that wills the End, muſt will the Means conducing to the Attainment of it*; the Effect to be produced being the *ultimate* End, and the Means the *ſubordinate* Ends which we have in View.--- And herein conſiſts the proper Notion of *Wiſdom*, viz. In *the right Judgment and Choice of Ends and Means*; *the beſt Ends and the fitteſt Means*; *and in a vigorous Activity in the Application of the Means in order to attain the End*.--- Thus it is in human Affairs; and from what we obſerve in the Courſe of Nature, in which there is an evident Subordination of Ends and Means, we unavoidably infer that there muſt be ſomething analogous to this in the Author of it, not becauſe He needs Means for Himſelf, but that He may make the Series or Courſe of Nature the more intelligible and inſtructive to us.--- Hence the beſt Part of the Study of Nature muſt conſiſt in the Diſcovery, as far as we are able, of what are called *final Cauſes*; *i. e.* of the plain Signatures of Deſign and Contrivance, and the Dependance and Connection of Ends and Means.

Of Matter and Form.

§ 8. In *artificial Effects*, or thoſe produced by Man, as in Building, *&c.* by reaſon of our Impotence we need *Matter* to work upon, and a *Form* or Model to work by, according to which the Effect, being framed or formed out of the pre-exiſtent Materials, is ſaid to conſiſt of Matter and Form; which have alſo been reckoned among the Cauſes, and they may each be called *Cauſa ſine quâ non*, as the Schoolmen uſed to ſpeak; but they cannot

be

be properly called Caufes, as having no Force or Defign in producing the Effect; we may, however, from hence, by Analogy, in fpeaking of other Things, advantageoufly make ufe of what is called, the *Ratio Materialis*, and *Formalis* of Things in Nature, and even of Things purely intellectual.---And becaufe we need *Matter* and *Form* in producing *artificial Effects*, we are apt to think, or at leaft to fpeak as tho' we thought, this the Method of the Almighty in producing *natural Effects*, but this is owing to our Weaknefs, whereby we are apt to meafure Him by ourfelves. Indeed he may be faid to have a Form, Idea, or *Archetype* in his infinite, all-comprehending Mind, conformable to which he acts; but this can mean no more than that all Things which he produceth are always prefent with Him, and perfectly known to Him, with all their Relations and Connections, antecedent to their Production, and that He produceth them conformable to His own Knowledge, Defign and Contrivance, being the Plan which he hath formed.---And that Exiftence of Things in the divine eternal Mind (if it may be fo called) as being perfectly known to Him, antecedent to their Production, is called their *Archetypal State*; and their Exiftence in *Rerum Natura*, as being actually produced by His Will and Power, and thereby perceived and known to us, is called their *Ectypal State*.

Of Effence, and Exiftence.

§ 9. To this Head therefore belongs the Diftinction between the *Effence* of Things, and their *Exiftence*.---By their *Effence*, we mean thofe conftituent Principles, Properties and Powers in them, which are neceffary to their Nature, as being what they are, whether confidered only as conceived in the Mind of an intelligent Being, or existing in *Rerum Natura*. Thus the Essence of *Gold* consists in its Colour, Weight, Fixedness, Ductility, Solubility in *Aqua Regia*, or whatever Properties are always found to co-exist in that Sort of Body which we call *Gold*, and no other: So the Essence of a *Rose* consists in such a particular Figure, Odour, *&c.*---of a *Man*, in an intelligent active Power, joined with an animal Body, of such a particular Shape, and Configuration of Parts:---of a *Triangle*, in three Sides, joining at three Angles:---of *Justice*, in rendering to every one his Due, *&c.*---In short, whatsoever goes to the *Definition* of a Thing, so as to give it a clear and necessary Discrimination from all other Things, we call the *Essence* of it, whether in fact it exist or not. Thus we have as clear an Idea of a *Rose* in Winter, as in *June*, when it is before our Eyes, and under our Noses; and as fixed and stable a Notion of a *Triangle*, *Circle*, *Justice*, or *Charity*, even upon Supposition that the Figures and Actions which go by those Names, do not exist in Nature or Fact, as if they did. Whereas by *Existence*, we generally mean a Thing's being actually in Fact and Nature, as well as in Idea or Conception, as a *Rose* in *June*, the *Sun* in the Firmament, a Man actually doing a just or kind Thing, *&c.*---Hence *Existence always implieth Essence*, tho' *Essence doth not necessarily imply Existence*, except in that of the necessarily existent Being, in whom Necessity of Existence is implied in His very Essence, and accordingly His original Name *JEHOVAH*, given by Himself, does literally signify, *The Essence existing*, as Mr. *Hutchinson* shews in *Mos. Sine Princip.* Ch. 2.

§ 10.

§ 10. In Purſuance of this Diſtinction between the *Eſſence* and *Exiſtence* of Things, which is neceſſary in order the better to conceive of them, it is here alſo needful to explain what we mean by the Word *Principle*, which originally ſignifies the *Beginning* of a Thing, or that from whence any Thing takes its Beginning, Origin, or Derivation; and in this Senſe it is nearly allied to the Word *Cauſe*. Thus God may be ſaid to be the *Principle* or Origin of all Things.---And as the eſſential Conſtituents whereof any Thing conſiſts, have been ranked among the Cauſes, they are alſo called the Principles of which it conſiſts, and into which it may, at leaſt in Conception, be reſolved; as Man of Soul and Body, Bodies of the four Elements, a Triangle of its three Sides and Angles, *&c.*-----And as the Properties and Powers of Things have been ſuppoſed to flow from their Eſſence; hence That in any Thing which is ſuppoſed to be the Foundation or Original from whence its Properties, Powers or Actions derive, is called the Principle of them; as Equality with two Right Angles from the Nature of a Triangle; Perception and Self-exertion from the Nature of the Soul, *&c.* And laſtly, as the Knowledge of Things conſiſts in underſtanding the Foundation of their Exiſtence, the Cauſes from whence they are derived, the Eſſentials whereof they conſiſt, and the Origin of their Properties and Powers; hence the Propoſitions expreſſive of this Knowledge, are called the Principles of any Science.

Of Principles.

§ 11. Under this Head of *Cauſes* and *Effects*, it is neceſſary more particularly to explain the Diſtinction of *Beings* into Things *neceſſary* and *con-*

Of Things neceſſary & contingent.

tingent

tingent.--By Things *contingent*, we mean, ſuch as depend on the free Exertion of the Wills and Powers of intelligent active Beings, and which therefore might not have been, had they ſo pleaſed, and conſequently their Exiſtence is precarious and dependent.---Thus, That I ſit here, and whether I ſhall ſit here an Hour longer, or not, is contingent, as depending on the Freedom of my own Will to do ſo, or not, as I pleaſe: Whether the Sun will riſe To-morrow, is contingent, as depending on the free Exertion of the Will of the Deity, who may, if he pleaſeth, this Moment put an End to the whole Courſe of Nature. And thus the Exiſtence of the whole Creation is contingent and precarious, as deriving from, and dependent on, the meer Will and Power of God, who if He pleaſed, might not have commanded Things into Being, and may ceaſe to Will their Continuance when He pleaſeth. Whereas by Things *neceſſary*, we mean ſuch as can't but be, which muſt be underſtood either with regard to our Power, or that of the Deity. Thus, with regard to our Power, it can't but be that Things are as they are, and as He hath made them, and that the Courſe of Nature proceeds as it does, and as He hath ordered it, which therefore, tho' not ſo in itſelf, to us is neceſſary and *Fate*. But that only is abſolutely neceſſary in itſelf, the Non-exiſtence of which would imply an Abſurdity and Contradiction; and nothing elſe is thus abſolutely neceſſary beſides the Deity Himſelf, the neceſſarily exiſtent Being, without whom nothing could ever have exiſted; and eternal Truths which are founded in the Perfection of his Nature, independent of any other Mind whatſoever; as, that the *Whole* is *bigger* than either *of its Parts*: That *all the Rays of every Circle are equal*: That

That *we ought to do as we would be done by.*--- Theſe, and the like, being abſolutely and unalterably neceſſary, antecedent to the Will, and independent of the Power of the Deity Himſelf, as well as His own Exiſtence and Perfections, muſt unavoidably be Emanations of that neceſſarily exiſtent Being.

Of Things finite and infinite.

§ 12. To this Head alſo belongs the Diſtinction of Beings into *Finite* and *Infinite*. That is ſaid to be *Finite*, which hath certain Limits or Bounds to its Exiſtence or Powers, as are all determinate Lines, and the Surfaces and Figures of Bodies, or the Powers of created Minds; in ſhort, all Kinds of Effects or Productions, which are limited to ſuch a Degree or Meaſure of Being, as their Cauſe is pleaſed to beſtow: For the Will and Power of the Cauſe that gives them Being, limits them to ſuch a Meaſure of Being, Extent and Power, as he thinks fit to impart; which, in many Inſtances, may be ſaid to be *Indefinite*, as extending vaſtly beyond our Comprehenſion. But *that Being* only is *Infinite* which comprehends all that truly *is*, without any Bounds or Limits, and whoſe Knowledge and Power extends to all that is, or is poſſible. Hence, * tho' the Word *Infinite*, in grammatical Conſtruction is a negative Term, uſed in Accommodation to our weak Capacities, yet what it expreſſeth is truly *poſitive*, as implying all that abſolutely *is*; and the Word *Finite*, is truly the *Negative*, as implying but a limited Part of that which truly is; the *Infinite* being the abſolute independent Being, or *Being* by way of Eminency, and without the Power of any other Being to limit or controul

* *Vide Cambray* on this Subject, in his Demonſtration.

controul it; and the *Finite*, intirely dependent on the Will and Power of another to be and continue what it is, and so exists only conditionally.

§ 13. To this Head of *Causes* and *Effects*, belongs also the Distinction of Things *possible* and *impossible*. We say a Thing is *possible*, when there is a Power sufficient to produce it, and impossible, when there is no Power adequate to the Production of it:---Of which some Things are *impossible* in their own Nature, as implying a Contradiction in themselves, as that there should be a *Mountain without Declivity*, or a *Triangle consisting only of two Sides*, which are impossible to God himself, not for want of Power in Him, but because they imply a Repugnancy in themselves, or a Contradiction to some necessary and eternal Truth, which God himself cannot alter. And of Things *possible* in their own Nature; some are possible to an unlimited Power, which yet are *impossible* to a Power that is limited: A Man can build a *House*, tho' he cannot create a *World*. And of limited Powers there is an endless Variety, so that what is possible to one may be impossible to another: Here therefore the Maxim is, That *what is Fact is possible*, but, *it does not therefore follow*, *that if it be possible it is Fact*.

Of Things possible and impossible.

§ 14. And lastly: To this Head of *Causes* and *Effects* doth also belong the Distinction of Things *perfect* and *imperfect*: An Effect is said to be *perfect*, when it is finished according to the Plan or Design of it, and fitted to answer the End proposed, from whence we arise to the general Notion of *Perfection*. And we say, a Being

Of Things perfect and imperfect.

ing or Thing is *perfect*, when it hath all the Parts, Properties or Powers, that a Thing of that Nature ought to have in order to conſtitute it in that Kind of Being, and to render it capable of anſwering the End of its being: As a Man is ſaid to be perfect, that has all the Parts and Powers that a Man, as ſuch, ought to have, ſo as to anſwer the general End of his Being; *i. e.* ſome good Degree of Happineſs:---He is then ſaid to be perfect in his Kind, tho' ſome of the ſame Kind may have their Properties and Powers in a greater Degree of Perfection than others, and ſo be perfecter in *Degree*, tho' not in *Kind*, and conſequently capable of anſwering ſome nobler Ends, with regard both to themſelves and others, as enjoying or communicating certain higher Degrees of Happineſs. On the other Hand, we ſay a Thing is *imperfect*, when it is deſtitute of certain Parts or Properties that a Thing of that Kind ought to have; as a Man with but one Hand, or one Eye, or an Ideot, *&c.* who conſequently cannot ſo well be uſeful to others, or enjoy himſelf. But if any Creature hath all the Parts and Properties that a Creature of that Kind ought to have, tho' it is ſaid to be *perfect* in its *Kind*, yet it is ſaid to be but *comparatively perfect* with reſpect to other Kinds of Beings of greater Perfection and Excellency, as being made for higher Ends; *i. e.* to enjoy or communicate greater Degrees of Happineſs; but what Degrees of Being or Perfection any Thing has, it receives from the free Will and Pleaſure of its Cauſe. And that Being only is ſaid to be *abſolutely perfect*, who hath an entire abſolute Fulneſs of Being, Perfection and Excellency, and conſequently enjoys the higheſt Happineſs, having in and of Himſelf

Himſelf all Being, all that truly is, and therefore an All-ſufficiency, even every Thing that can contribute to render both Himſelf and all his Creatures compleatly happy.

Of Truth and Good.

§ 15. To this Head of *Perfection* therefore belong the Notions of *Truth* and *Good*. A Thing is ſaid to be *true* with reſpect to the original Archetype, Plan or Deſign of it, or ſo much of Being or Perfection as it was deſigned to partake of, and *Good* with reſpect to the End of it, which it was deſigned to anſwer: So that its *Truth* conſiſteth in its Conformity to its Plan or Archetype, which is its Standard; and its *Goodneſs* is its Fitneſs to anſwer its End. And as the Plan is formed with a View at the End to be anſwered, they are in effect only the ſame Thing under diverſe Conſiderations; and a Thing is *True*, conſidered as intelligible, and *Good* as eligible. Thus a *Houſe* is ſaid to be *True*, as it anſwers its Archetype or Model, as conceiv'd or underſtood in the Mind of the Architect; and *Good*, as it is fitted to anſwer the End he deſigned in it, *viz.* the Convenience and Pleaſure of its Inhabitant, on which it is delightful or eligible. So the *Truth* of each *Creature*, and of the whole *World*, conſiſts in its Conformity to its original Deſign, Archetype or Standard, conceived in the infinite Mind of the great divine Architect, and as ſuch, intelligible to Him, and in ſome Meaſure to any other Mind; and its *Goodneſs* conſiſts in its Fitneſs to anſwer His Ends in giving it Being, and particulary the Happineſs of His rational Creatures, on account of which, it is pleaſing and eligible to Him, or any other intelligent Being, that feels or diſcerns that Fitneſs. Hence Goodneſs being in effect the ſame

ſame with Perfection, muſt have the ſame Diſtinctions of *Kind* and *Degree*, *Comparative* and *Abſolute* as above. And the infinite Mind of the Deity is the Standard of all Things that exiſt, He is the *Truth* itſelf abſolutely and by way of Eminence, comprehending in Himſelf all that is and can be; all Reality and Perfection, conſidered as intelligible and variouſly imitable in and by his Creatures: And as He is the Pattern and Author of all Fitneſs and Proportion to any End, and the Fountain of all that is pleaſant and beatifying, or the Original of all that is Good in the whole Creation, He is *Goodneſs* itſelf, and therefore infinitely eligible, and to be choſen and loved above all Things. Thus we are led from the *Type* to the *Archetype*; from all the Emanations of *Truth* and *Good* in the Creature, variouſly portioned out as pleaſed Him, to that Being who is the great Principle and Original of all; the *Truth* itſelf, even all *Truth*; and *Good* itſelf, the chief *Good*, the ΤΟ 'ΑΓΑΘΟ'Ν; infinite *Truth*, and infinite *Good*, all that can beatify both Intellect, Will and Affection.

Of Beauty and Harmony.

§ 16. To this Head of *Perfection* or *Excellency* we may alſo refer the Conſideration of *Beauty* and *Harmony*, which have a manifeſt Relation to ſome End which any Thing is deſigned for. By *Beauty*, we vulgarly mean, ſuch an Aſſemblage of viſible Ideas as pleaſes and charms the Eye; and by *Harmony*, ſuch an Aſſemblage of Sounds as pleaſes and charms the Ear. But, more ſtrictly ſpeaking, it is the Mind or Intellect that is charmed on theſe Occaſions, by Means of the Objects of Sight and Hearing. What is it then that is *Beauty* and *Harmony* to the interior intellectual

lectual Senſe of the Mind? And if it be duly conſidered, it will be always found that it is Fitneſs and Proportion, either real or apparent, in relation to ſome End or Uſe, in thoſe Objects that pleaſe and charm us. Thus in *Beauty*; an Aſſemblage of various Ideas, all fitted and proportioned to each other, and, in the Whole, to one uniform Deſign and End, ſubſervient to the Advantage and Pleaſure of an intelligent Mind, or of a ſocial Syſtem of intelligent Beings; this is what pleaſes and charms under the Notion of Beauty, as might be exemplified in the Beauty of a Perſon, an Animal, or a Building, *&c.* And from ſenſible Things it is figuratively and by Analogy transferred to Affections, Actions and Behaviour; the Beauty whereof conſiſteth in their uniform Fitneſs and Tendency to the Order, Peace and Happineſs of each individual Mind, and, in the Whole, of any ſocial Syſtem: So as to *Harmony*; it is an Aſſemblage of various Sounds, all fitted and proportioned to each other, and in the whole Compoſition, to an uniform Deſign and End, expreſſive of what may pleaſe and delight the Mind: And from Muſic it is transferred to ſignify Things fitted and proportioned to each other, and to the whole Syſtem, and thence pleaſing and delightful, whether it be in the natural or moral World. Hence we ſpeak of the Harmony and Order of all Nature, and of the Harmony and Order of Society. So that both in *Beauty* and *Harmony*, the Fitneſs and Proportion of Things, Affections and Actions to each other, and in the Whole, to the Pleaſure, Peace and Happineſs of intelligent Beings, is always underſtood. And from thence we ariſe to the Apprehenſion of the firſt original *Beauty*, the TO

KAAON,

ΚΑΛΟΝ, the Pattern and Source of all Fitneſs and Proportion in the abſolute Perfection of the divine Intellect and Conduct, and the *Harmony* of the divine Attributes and Operations, and all the Happineſs, both divine, human and angelical, reſulting therefrom.

Of Subſtances and Accidents, Subjects & Adjuncts.

§ 17. NEXT to the Conſideration of a Being or Thing as exiſting from its Cauſes, we conſider it as a *Subſtance* with regard to its *Accidents*, and a *Subject* with reſpect to its *Adjuncts*. The primary Notion we have of *Subſtance* is taken from *Body*, as being ſomething that is *hard* or *ſolid*, and reſiſts the Touch, as *Gold*, *Wood*, &c. and obſerving a Number of other Ideas or *ſenſible Qualities* always attending it, or connected with it, we call them its *Accidents*, as *long*, *broad*, *thick*, *ſquare*, *round*, *red*, *blue*, *yellow*, &c. Of theſe, we obſerve ſome eſſential to all *Bodies*, as *Length*, *Breadth*, *Thickneſs*; others we obſerve to be various in different Bodies, as *ſquare*, *round*, *white*, *black*, &c. Thoſe *Qualities* that are eſſential to any Thing, we call *Properties*; and the others are more properly called *Accidents*, *Modes* or Modifications. Now that *ſolid*, *extended*, figured Thing, which reſiſts the Touch, being the firſt Idea or Combination of Ideas, to which we give the Name *Subſtance*, we are apt to conſider *that* as the Foundation or *Subſtratum* to the reſt, and the other Qualities as ſubſiſting in it, or depending on it, tho', ſtrictly ſpeaking, they are rather only co-exiſtent and connected with it by the Law of Nature, which is the meer *Fiat* of the Almighty. This is our original and proper Notion of *Subſtance* in *Bodies*, and from thence we analogically apply it to

Minds or Spirits, tho' they are Beings of an intirely different Kind, and have nothing common to them but meer *Being* or Existence, so that great Care must be taken that we do not imagine any Thing like a solid *Substratum* in Spirits as such. But if we must apply the Word *Substance* indifferently to both, it may be defined to mean any distinct *Being* considered as consisting of its *essential Properties*. Thus a *Body* we call a *Substance*, as consisting of *solid Length*, *Breadth* and *Thickness*, or solid Extension, which are its essential Properties, without which it cannot be conceived as being what it is: So we call a *Spirit* or *Mind*, a Substance, as being a *Power* or *Principle* of *conscious Perception* and *Activity*, which are Properties essential to it as being what it is. Thus we may say, a *Tree*, a *Horse*, a *Man*, an *Angel*, &c. (and by Analogy, even the *Deity* Himself) are Substances. And those *Qualities* that are not essential to it, may, as I said, be called its *Modes* or *Accidents*; as in a *Man*, to be *tall* or *short*, *white* or *black*, *fat* or *lean*, *learned* or *ignorant*, *virtuous* or *vicious*, &c. which have also, sometimes, been called *Adjuncts*: But this Term is more properly applied to external Appendages or Circumstances, as *Clothes*, *Riches*, &c. with respect to which the Being is called a *Subject*; and any of them, whether Properties, Modes or Adjuncts, in speaking of it, are called *Attributes*; and a succinct lively Enumeration of any or all of these, in any Subject, discriminating it from any other Thing, is called a *Description* of it.

Of Time and Place, Space and Duration.

§ 18. EVERY *Body* or sensible Thing that is, must necessarily have some *Time* and *Place*, in which it exists, which are reckoned among its principal Modes; and by its *Time*, is usually

uſually meant, that Portion of *Duration*; and by its *Place* is meant, that Portion of *Space*, in which it exiſts. But then by *Space*, we muſt mean the whole Extent of ſenſible Things, the *Place* of each particular Thing, being that Part of the whole Extent which it occupies, in its proper Situation relative to the reſt: And by *Duration*, muſt be meant, the whole Continuance of the Exiſtence of the entire ſenſible World, meaſured out by the Revolutions of the Sun; and the *Time* of any particular ſenſible Thing, means, its continuing to exiſt during ſo many Parts, or ſuch a Number of his Revolutions. But *Time*, conſidered as a Conception in the Mind, is nothing elſe but the Succeſſion of its Ideas, of which the Succeſſion of ſome principal Ones, as the Revolution of *Years*, *Days*, &c. being ſettled and ſtable according to the eſtabliſhed Courſe of Nature, are conſidered as Standards or Meaſures to the reſt. Such are Time and Place, Space and Duration, literally with regard to the ſenſible World, to which they properly belong, and they are only figuratively, and by Analogy, aſcribed to Spirits or intelligent active Beings, concerning which the Term *Ubi*, *where*, and *when*, by ſome have been preferred. For, as their Exiſtence is intirely of another Kind from that of Bodies, ſo muſt their Space and Duration be: As their Exiſtence conſiſts in conſcious, active Intelligence, ſo their Space muſt mean only the Extent or Reach of their intelligent active Powers, and their Duration only their Continuance to exert thoſe Powers: But, ſtrictly ſpeaking, they are ſo far from exiſting in Space and Time, that, on the other Hand, Space and Time do truly exiſt in them. And accordingly the infinite eternal Mind is ſo far from existing in infinite Space and Duration, that He comprehendeth all Space and Duration, and every Thing that is, within His boundless Intellect, and is present to all Times and Places, not after the Manner of being co-extended with them, but as an infinitely active, all-comprehending Intellect, to whom all Things, all Times and Places, are at once present, without Succession or Limitation; *i. e.* they are at once known to His infinite Mind, and subjected to, and dependent upon, His unlimited Will and Power.

Of Whole and Parts.

§ 19. Next to the Consideration of a Being or Thing, as a Substance with regard to its Accidents, and a Subject with regard to its Adjuncts, we consider it as a *Whole* with regard to the Parts whereof it consists: As a *Man* consists of *Soul* and *Body*; and his *Body*, of his *Head*, *Trunk* and *Limbs*, each of which may be yet further sub-divided. On the other Hand, we call that a *Part*, which is considered as being not an entire Thing of itself, but as it goes, in Conjunction with other Parts, to the Constitution of a *Whole* or entire Being, as a *Leg* or an *Arm*, with respect to the *Human Body*: Such is any individual Thing with respect to the Parts whereof it consists, which therefore may be called an *Individual Whole*, as not being divisible into more of the same Kind, or Quantity, and the Parts of which are not of themselves intire Beings. But besides this, there is, what is called an *aggregate Whole*, the Parts of which, are each a distinct intire Being, tho' it has a Relation to other distinct Beings, with which it is connected as Parts of another Whole; and the Parts are either of the *same*, or of *different Kinds*: Such, of the first Sort, is an *Army*, consisting of the many distinct

diſtinct individual Men whereof it is conſtituted, each of which, is an intire Being of himſelf, and all of the *ſame* Kind.----And ſuch, of the other Sort, is the whole *World* with regard to all the various diſtinct Beings whereof it conſiſts, but thoſe of *different* Kinds, as *Bodies*, *Spirits*, *Men*, *Beaſts*, *Trees*, *Stones*, &c. So that the ſame Thing may be a *Whole* with regard to the Parts whereof it conſiſts, and a *Part*, as it goes to the Conſtitution of another Whole: And the Maxim here is, that *The Whole is greater than either of its Parts, and equal to them all taken together*, which is the Foundation of all mathematical Demonſtrations. This Notion of *Whole* and *Parts*, is originally taken from *Bodies*, and is properly and literally to be underſtood of them and their Dimenſions, but may analogically and improperly be applied alſo to *Spirits*; in which Senſe we may ſay, The *Soul* is a *Whole*, and the *Underſtanding*, *Will*, *Affections* and *Exertions* of it may be conſidered as Parts of it, they bearing the like Analogy to the Soul, as the Members and Organs do to the Body.

Of Unity and Multiplicity, Number and Order.

§ 20. UNDER this Head of *Whole* and *Parts*, we may conſider the Notions of *Unity* and *Multiplicity*, *Number* and *Order*. A *Whole* or *intire Being*, conſidered as being *ſimple* or indiviſible into more of the ſame Kind or Quantity, we call a *Unit* or One intire individual Being, as one *Shilling*, one *Tree*, one *Ox*, one *Man*, one *Angel*: Thence it is applied alſo to an aggregate Whole, as one *Army*, one *World*. And the Parts of which any Whole is compounded or conſiſts, are ſaid to be *manifold*. And by how much the leſs of Compoſition there is in any Being, by ſo much the perfecter it is, as being ſo much the more One: Hence *Spirit* being compounded only of Power and Act, is more perfect than *Body*, which is compounded of many Parts and Dimenſions. And as Power and Act in the *Deity* intirely coincide, He is the moſt perfect Being, as being the moſt ſimple and intirely *One*, and therefore is called *pure Act*, without any Variety or Multiplicity; a moſt perfect *Unit*, conſiſting of all Reality and Perfection. Now from the *Multiplicity* of Individuals with regard to an aggregate Whole, and of Parts with Regard to each individual Whole, we have the Conception of *Number*, the Parts being numerous or conſiſting of a Number of Units, as *many Members* in the ſame Body, *many Men*, *many Beaſts*, *many Trees*, &c. to which in Computation, we give the Denominations of *One*, *Two*, *Three*, *Four*, &c. And theſe Parts we conſider as ſubſiſting in ſome *Order*, according to their ſeveral Relations and Situations, with regard to each other, and to the Whole: Of which we ſay, one is *prior*, the other *poſterior* to the other, either in *Nature*, *Time*, *Place*, *Dignity* or *Knowledge*, as a *Father* to his *Son*, &c. And this Order of Things which we expreſs by the Terms, *firſt*, *ſecond*, *third*, *fourth*, &c. we find to be founded in ſome Eſtabliſhment which we obſerve to be made in the Courſe of Nature, which therefore, in all our Diviſions and Sub-diviſions, Conceptions and Reaſonings, we ſhould make our Standard, and endeavour to follow it as exactly as ever we can.

Of Identity and Diverſity.

§ 21. MOREOVER, to this Head of Unity and Multiplicity, belong the Notions of *Identity* and *Diverſity*. A Thing is ſaid to be one and the *ſame*, when it appears to have all the eſſential individuating

viduating Properties at one Time that it had at another, tho' it may differ in ſome Things accidental or circumſtantial, as a Man at 5 and at 50: But if Things differ in any Thing eſſential, we ſay, they are *Diverſe*, being not the ſame; but the one a different and diſtinct Being from the other; as an *Apple* and an *Oyſter*. But *Identity* is of very different Conſideration in *Bodies* and in *Spirits*, as they are Beings of an entirely different Kind. In *Bodies*, we call that *one* and the *ſame*, which, however it may differ in ſome Things not eſſential to it, yet in Things peculiar to it, it affects our Senſes in the ſame Manner at one Time as at another, or conſiſts of the ſame ſenſible Qualities, *Figure*, *Colour*, &c. eſſential to it; as a *Mountain* now, and twenty Years ago: And thoſe are *diverſe* or diſtinct Bodies one from another, that conſiſt of different ſenſible Qualities eſſential to each, as *Gold* and *Lead*; or that in Bodies is the ſame or different, which appears to conſiſt of the ſame or different individuating ſenſible Qualities. But as by a *Spirit*, which is alſo called a *Perſon*, we mean a diſtinct, conſcious, intelligent Agent, ſo his Identity conſiſts in being conſcious of a Series of Perceptions and Actions that he knows to be his own and not another's, by which therefore he knows he is the ſame Perſon now with himſelf twenty or fifty Years ago, which continued Conſciouſneſs is his diſtinct individuating Property. Whereas *Peter* is not the ſame with *Paul*, but another Perſon, each having diſtinct individuating Properties, the one being conſcious of a different and diſtinct Series of Perceptions and Actions from the other: And another appears to me the ſame with himſelf at different Times, or to be a different Perſon, according as from his Words and Actions, he appears to be conscious or not conscious of the same Perceptions and Actions. This is the usual and common Sense of the Word *Person*, which, however, is sometimes used to signify not a distinct Being, but a distinct Capacity: In which Sense the same Intelligence may sustain diverse Persons, by acting in so many different Characters or Capacities. I need say nothing here of the Sense of this Word, as used *in Divinis*.

Of Things agreeing or opposite.

§ 22. FURTHERMORE, some Things are said to *agree*, others to *differ*, and be *opposite* to each other: And *those Things that agree in a third Thing, are said to agree between themselves*; and *the Idea or Conception of the one, in some respect, includes or implies the Idea or Conception of the the other, and vice versâ*. Thus Things are said to *agree* in their Causes, Effects, Properties, Subjects, Adjuncts, Time, Place, Quantity, Quality, &c. As *two Sons* have one common Parent, *two Men* are contemporary, or are Countrymen, or have the same Occupation, &c. But Things are said to *disagree* or differ in relation to these Things, as two Men to be of different Countries or Occupations, &c. And to be *opposite*, when they are contrary the one to the other, and the Idea or Notion of the one excludes that of the other, as *Light* and *Darkness*, *Heat* and *Cold*, *Extension* and *Thought*, *True* and *False*, *Right* and *Wrong*, &c. and any Thing and its *Privation* or *Negation*, as *Sight* and *Blindness*, &c.

Of Things equal or unequal.

§ 23. IN the *next* Place, we say, Things are *equal*, when they have the same *Quantity*, whether *discreet* or *continued*; *i. e. Number* or *Magnitude*, as as $2+2=4$ and any two *Right Angles* are equal to each other, having the ſame, or an equal Number of Parts or Degrees. On the contrary, we ſay Things are *Unequal*, when one is *Greater*, and the other *Leſs*, as 3 is more than 2, a *Right Angle* is *greater* than an *Acute*, and *leſs* than an *Obtuſe*, &c. And here the Mathematicians have ſeveral Maxims which are the Foundations of their Demonſtrations; as, *Equals added to Equals, make the Whole equal*; and *Equals taken from Equals, leave the Remainder equal:* So of *Unequals*, &c. And from *Bodies* and their Dimenſions, this is by Analogy transferred to *Spirits* or Minds, which are compared in their Powers and Faculties, as Bodies, *&c.* in their Quantities: Thus we ſay, one *Man* or *Angel* has an equal, greater or leſs Degree of Underſtanding, Force or Activity, than another, and thoſe of the Deity are infinite, and beyond all Compariſon. To this Head belong the Arguments, *a majore ad minus affirmando*, and *a minore ad majus negando*; as, if one Man can lift ſuch a Weight, much more two; and if two cannot lift it, much leſs one.

Of Things like and unlike.

§ 24. AND *laſtly*, we ſay, Things are *like* one another, when the one reſembleth the other in ſome Quality, Power or Faculty; and of all other *Analogies*, thoſe between the *natural* and *moral* World are the moſt pleaſant and uſeful; GOD having deſigned the one as an Emblem of the other, whereby we may be beſt inſtructed from our Senſes in what moſt concerns us: As *Knowledge is like Light*, or *Benevolence like Attraction*; i. e. *Knowledge* is to the *Mind*, what *Light* is to the *Eye*, in the Diſcovery of *Truth*. In like Manner, *Benevolence* is to *Society* what *Attraction*

is

is to *Nature*, as the one preſerves Order and Harmony in the natural World; ſo the other preſerves Peace and Happineſs in the moral World. This is what is called *Analogy* or *Proportion*; and is either *continued* or *disjunct*.---*Continued* when the *firſt* Term is to the *ſecond*, as the *ſecond* is to the *third*, as, The *Parent* is to the *Child*, as the *Child* is to the *Grandchild*. *Disjunct*, when the *firſt* is to the *ſecond*, as the *third* to the *fourth*; as, *Virtue* is to the *Soul*, as *Health* is to the *Body*, in regard to Eaſe and Tranquility.---- To this Head belong the Mathematicians Doctrine of Proportions, or the Similitude of Ratio's, as, 2 : 4 : : 4 : 8. and 2 : 4 : : 6 : 12.-----Here likewiſe belong moral Proportions, or the Fitneſs of Affections and Actions to Characters with regard to Happineſs. Hence that reciprocal Proportion expreſſing the grand Foundation Principle of Morals, That ſuch Affections and Actions as are right or wrong in another towards me, as tending to promote my Happineſs or Miſery in the Whole, muſt for the ſame Reaſon be right or wrong in me towards him, ſuppoſing an Exchange of Characters.---Thus of *Similitude*. On the other Hand, we ſay, Things are *Unlike*, when they have different Qualities and Powers; as *John* is not like *Thomas*, the one being a good Genius, the other a Dunce.

Of Denomination & Definition.

§ 25. WHATEVER Being or Thing, or whatever Power, Effect, Property, Adjunct or Part, Quantity or Quality of any Thing be the Object of our Conſideration; in order the better to think of it by ourſelves, and eſpecially in order to converſe with one another about it, it is neceſſary to give it a *Name*, or annex ſome Sound or or other Sign, agreed upon to be ſteadily ſignificative of it, whether it be an Object of the Senſe and Imagination, or of the pure Intellect and Reaſon; and that Sound or Sign ſo eſtabliſhed, becomes a Kind of Vehicle to the Idea or Conception, whether Simple, Compound or Complex. Thus we give the Names *White*, *Black*, *Red*, &c. to the Colours ſo called, *Hard*, *Soft*, *Hot*, *Cold*, &c. to the tangible Qualities ſo called; and *Conſciouſneſs*, *Perception*, *Self-exertion*, &c. to the ſimple Conceptions ſo called.---Thus to inſtance in the Compounds; we give the Name *Gold* to a certain yellow Metal that is the heavieſt and moſt ductile of all others, and the Name *Cherry* to the Fruit of ſuch a Tree, and of ſuch a particular Figure, Conſiſtence and Taſte; and ſo the Name *Juſtice*, to an Action of an intelligent Agent, deſigning to render to every one what he apprehends to be his Due, *&c.* This is called *Denomination*, or giving Names to Things: And the great Rule to be obſerved in this Affair, is, That we conſtantly annex ſuch an Idea or Conception, or ſuch a preciſe Collection or Combination of either ſenſible Ideas or intellectual Notions, to ſuch a Name or Word, and always uſe it in the ſame Senſe. And the true Notion of a *Definition*, whether in Things ſenſible or intellectual, conſiſts in explaining what are the preciſe Ideas or Conceptions, which are combined and annexed to ſuch a Name. Thus the Word *Gold* means a yellow fuſible Body, of the greateſt Weight and Ductility of any other, and ſoluble in *Aqua Regia*. So the Word *Spirit*, means a conſcious, intelligent, active, ſelf-exerting Being. Thus we define compound Ideas, or complex Conceptions; but as for thoſe that are ſimple,

they

they cannot be defined otherwiſe than by ſome ſynonymous Term, becauſe they can be known only by Experience.

Of Abſtraction, and of Individuals, Sorts and Kinds.

§ 26. Any one intire Being that cannot be divided into more of the ſame Kind, we call an *Individual*, whether it be a *Body*, or a *Spirit*, and in order the better to think and ſpeak of it, we give it a proper Name, as, to this *Man* the Name of *John*, to that, *Peter*; to this *Horſe*, the Name *Bucephalus*, to that *Dog*, the Name *Argus*, &c. And if there be no Occaſion for a proper Name, we ſay *this Tree*, *that Stone*, that *Piece of Gold*, &c. And obſerving that there are a great Number of *Individuals* that agree in certain eſſential Properties that diſcriminate them from all other Things, we call all the Beings of that Sort, a *Species*, and agree upon a common Name that ſhall indifferently ſtand for every Individual of that Sort: This is what is meant by *Abſtraction*. Thus obſerving all the Individuals of *Men* to agree in a certain Figure, Shape and Structure, and in certain Powers of Reaſon, Speech and Activity, we call the whole Species by the general Name, *Man*, in which we do, in effect, ſubſtitute ſome individual Idea to repreſent the whole Species, and annex to it a general Name common to all the Individuals. And comparing this Sett of Beings, which we call *Mankind*, with another Sett which we call *Beaſts*, we find there are ſome Properties in which they all agree, as Life, Senſe and ſpontaneous Motion, *&c.* to theſe we give a more general Name or *Genus*, that ſhall ſtand for them all, as the Word *Animal*. And aſcending higher, we obſerve that each Tribe of *Animals*

agree

agree with another Sett of Beings called *Plants*, in vegetable Life, and ſo conſtitute a yet more general Name to ſtand for them all, as the Word *Animate*. And finding all theſe agree ſtill with a vaſtly greater Number of other Things, *Elements*, *Stones*, *Metals*, &c. in the three Dimenſions, Length, Breadth and Thickneſs, we agree on the yet more general Name *Body* to comprehend them all. And laſtly, *Spirits* are yet another Sett of Beings, intirely and *toto Cœlo* different from *Bodies* of any Sort, whoſe Eſſence conſiſts in conſcious Perception and Activity, and have nothing common with them but bare Exiſtence; ſo that we comprehend them all, both *Bodies* and *Spirits*, both Things perceiving, and Things perceived, Things active, and Things paſſive, under the moſt general Name *Being*, or *Thing*; *i. e.* what is, or exiſts. This is the higheſt *Genus* of all, which, with the ſubordinate *Genera* or Kinds, have been conſidered as another Kind of *Whole*, called *Totum Genericum* (to diſtinguiſh it from the other *Whole*, explained above, § 19. which is properly ſo called, but for Diſtinction-ſake is alſo termed *Totum Integrale*) and its Parts are called *Species* (the Parts of the other being called its Members.)----And the *Diviſion* of the *Genus* into its Species may more fitly be called *Diſtribution*, and that of the *Integrum* into its *Members*, *Partition*. Thus in the Inſtance before us, we diſtribute *Beings* into *Bodies* and *Spirits*; *Bodies* into *Inanimate* and *Animate*; *Animate* into *Plants* and *Animals*; and *Animals* into *Men* and *Beaſts*. And laſtly, theſe loweſt *Species* can be diſtributed only into the ſeveral *Individuals*: But the *Individuals*, tho' they cannot be *diſtributed* into *Sorts*, they may be *diſtinguiſhed* by their

Cauſes

Causes, *Effects*, *Subjects* or *Adjuncts*, &c. as, by their *Families*, *Places*, or *Countries*, by their *Colours*, *Sects* or *Occupations*, and other accidental Circumstances.

§ 27. *Particularly of Bodies and Spirits.* It is of great Importance, in order to think clearly and justly, to take Care that we have as exact a Notion as possible of all those Properties in every Kind of Being, that do essentially distinguish one from another, that we may make our *Definitions* and *Divisions* just, and avoid as far as possible, that Perplexity of Thought and Expression which ariseth from confounding one Thing with another. But this is more especially necessary in that first great Division of *Beings* into *Bodies* and *Spirits*; because we take our first Rise to Knowledge from sensible Things or Bodies, and by that Means are so prepossessed with a Notion of their Reality and Importance, that it is with much Difficulty that we rise to the Notion of Spirits and what relates to them; or, when we do, to have any strong Apprehension of their Reality and Importance, or to conceive of them but under corporeal Images. We should therefore labour much in the Business of Reflexion, and Abstraction from sensible to intellectual Things, and disengage ourselves from Sense and Imagination as much as possible; and consider, that tho' our Notion of Spirits is intirely of a different Nature and Original, from that of Bodies, it is neither less real and substantial, nor indeed less clear and certain. These we have from Sense and Imagination, and those from Consciousness and Reasoning; but as these are Faculties of as much Reality and Certainty, as those (nay more) we are not less certain

tain of the Exiſtence of Spirits than of Bodies, nor have we a leſs clear Notion of the one than the other. I am as intuitively certain of my own Exiſtence by Conſciouſneſs, as of the Exiſtence of Bodies by Senſe, and am as demonſtratively ſure of the Exiſtence of other Spirits, and eſpecially of the eternal Parent Mind, as I am of any Thing imaginable, whatſoever: Nay (as I ſaid) upon due Conſideration, it will appear that the Evidence and Reality here hath much the Advantage. And I do as clearly and perfectly know what I mean, when I ſay *I* or *myſelf*, as when I ſay *my Body*; and have as clear a Notion of the Meaning or Conceptions annexed to the Words, *Senſe*, *Imagination*, *Conſciouſneſs*, *Underſtanding*, *Reaſon*, *Pleaſure*, *Averſion*, *Activity*, *Self-exertion*, &c. as of the Meaning or Ideas annexed to the Words, *Extenſion*, *Figure*, *Solidity*, *Motion*, *Colour*, *Sound*, *Heat*, *Cold*, *Sweet*, *Bitter*, &c. I as perfectly know the one as the other. So that I muſt conſider *Spirits*, as being as much real and intelligible Beings as *Bodies*, tho' of entirely a different Kind; and indeed as much more real, as they are a more perfect Kind of Beings; as Perception and Action are Things of greater Reality and Perfection, than being perceived and acted; Activity than Paſſivity: And they muſt be of as much more Importance, as one's *Self* and the Enjoyment of one's Self is of more Importance to us, than any outward ſenſible Objects.

Of Signs, Metaphor & Analogy.

§ 28. INDEED there is a Difficulty in being duly diſengaged from Things *ſenſible*, in order the better to conceive of Things *intelligible*, *ſpiritual* and *divine*, and we are obliged to make uſe of thoſe

thoſe as a Means and Step to theſe, uſing ſenſible *Signs*, *Metaphors* and *Analogies*, to repreſent and ſhadow forth thoſe more noble, abſtract Objects of Intellect, Reaſon and Faith: For (to uſe the Words of the great Author of the *Minute Philoſopher*, Dial. VII. § 16.) "As the Mind " is better acquainted with ſome Sort of Objects " which are earlier ſuggeſted to it, ſtrike it more " ſenſibly, or are more eaſily comprehended " than others, it is naturally led to ſubſtitute theſe " Objects for ſuch as are more ſubtil, fleeting " or difficult to conceive. Nothing, I ſay, is " more natural than to make the Things we " know, a Step to thoſe we do not know; and " to repreſent and explain Things leſs familiar, by " others that are more ſo. Now it is certain " we imagine before we reflect, and we perceive " by Senſe before we imagine, and of all our " Senſes, the Sight is the moſt clear, diſtinct, " various, agreeable and comprehenſive. Hence " it is natural to aſſiſt the Intellect by Imagina- " tion, the Imagination by Senſe, and the other " Senſes by Sight. Hence Figures, Metaphors " and Types. We illuſtrate ſpiritual Things by " corporeal; we ſubſtitute Sounds for Thoughts, " and written Letters for Sounds; Emblems, " Symbols and Hieroglyphics, for Things too " obſcure to ſtrike, and too various or too fleet- " ing to be retained: We ſubſtitute Things ima- " ginable for Things intelligible; ſenſible Things " for imaginable; ſmaller Things for thoſe too " great to comprehend eaſily, and greater Things " for ſuch as are too ſmall to be diſcerned di- " ſtinctly; preſent Things for abſent; perma- " nent for periſhing; and viſible for inviſible. " Hence the Uſe of Diagrams: Hence Right

Lines

" Lines are ſubſtituted for Time, Velocity and
" other Things of very different Natures. Hence
" we ſpeak of Spirits in a figurative Stile, ex-
" preſſing the Operations of the Mind by Allu-
" ſions and Terms borrowed from ſenſible
" Things, ſuch as, *apprehend*, *conceive*, *reflect*,
" *diſcourſe*, and the like. And hence thoſe Al-
" legories which illuſtrate Things intellectual by
" Viſions exhibited to the Fancy."---Hence alſo
it is that we conceive and ſpeak of God Almighty by *Analogy* from the greateſt Perfections in
ourſelves, ſuch as *Knowledge*, *Wiſdom*, *Power*,
Juſtice, *Goodneſs*, &c. which we ſubſtitute to repreſent his infinite Perfections, removing all Limitation and Imperfection.---And hence it is that
in the Revelation which God hath made of himſelf, and his Diſpenſations towards Mankind, he
cloaths himſelf with human Parts and Paſſions, in
order to render himſelf in ſome Meaſure intelligible to us, and moreover, teacheth us, what (to
all practical Purpoſes, which are chiefly aimed at)
it concerneth us to know of him and his Dealings with us, by Things and Relations familiar
among our ſelves, ſuch as, the Sun, Light and
Life, *Father*, *Son* and *Spirit*, *Mediator*, *Redeemer*,
Prieſt, *Propitiation*, *King*, *Kingdom*, &c. All which
gracious Accommodations to our low Capacities,
we muſt always ſo underſtand and explain as to
imply nothing contradictious or unworthy of his
infinite Excellency, implied in either his natural
or moral Perfections.---Thus much of the Mind's
ſimple Apprehenſion of its Objects, and their Relations, ariſing from our comparing them one with
another, and the Manner of our conceiving and
expreſſing them.

CHAP. III.

Of the Mind *judging*, *affirming*, *denying*, *assenting*, &c.

§ 1. I PROCEED now in the *second* Place to the Consideration of that Act of the Mind, which is called Judgment, *i. e.* which affirms or denies one Thing of another, and judges of True and False.---Accordingly I observe further: That no sooner hath the Mind compared its Ideas or Conceptions one with another, but, perceiving, or apprehending that it perceives their Connections and Repugnances, or the Agreement or Disagreement between them, it passeth some Judgment affirming or denying the one of the other, according as it apprehends the one is or is not included or implied in the other or connected with it. Thus observing the Ideas we call *Roundness* or *Brightness* agree with, or are included in the Idea to which we give the Name *Sun*, we affirm the *Sun* is *Round* or *Bright*.---And finding the Idea we call a *Square* is not comprehended in that of the *Sun*, we deny that *the Sun is Square*.---So with Regard to intellectual Notions; we affirm *Virtue is preferable to Gold*, and deny that *Riches are of so much Worth as Learning*; where *Excellency* beyond that of Gold is included in the Notion of *Virtue*, and an *Excellency* equal to that of *Learning* is not included in that of *Riches*.---These *Judgments* of the Mind expressed in Words, we call *Propositions*: And the Idea or Conception of which we affirm or deny

Of Judgments and Propositions.

ny any Thing, is called the *Subject* of the Propoſition; and that which is affirmed or denied of, it is called the *Attribute* or *Predicate*, and what joins them is the Verb; and what ſeparates them is the negative Particle; as, *the Sun* is *the Center*, or, is not *the Center of the World.*

Of Propoſitions univerſal, particular and ſingular.

§ 2. IN all Propoſitions the Subject is either a *General* or an *Individual* Idea or Conception.---If the Subject be a *general* Term, then it is either a *univerſal* or *particular* Propoſition.---It is a *univerſal Propoſition* when the Attribute or Predicate is underſtood to be affirmed or denied of all the Individuals contained under the Subject; as, *Man is a rational Creature*, *Man is not immortal*; and is generally expreſſed by ſome Term of Univerſality, *all* or *none*.---*All* is a *univerſal Affirmative*, as, *all Men are mortal*; and it is denied by denying the Term of Univerſality; as, *not all Men are mortal*; or by a particular Negative, as, *ſome Men are not mortal.*---*None* is a *univerſal Negative*, as, *no Vice is to be indulged*; which is denied by a particular Affirmative, as, *ſome Vice is to be indulged.*---On the other Hand, a Propoſition is *particular*, when the Predicate is underſtood to be affirmed or denied of only ſome of the Individuals contained under the Subject; as, *ſome Men are wiſe*, *ſome Men are not rich:* And a *particular Affirmative* is denied by a univerſal Negative; as, *no Men are wiſe*; and a *particular Negative* is denied by a univerſal Affirmative; as, *all Men are rich.*---But if the Subject be an Individual, the Propoſition is called *ſingular*, as *John is wiſe*, or *is not rich*, which are denied, the One, by ſaying, *he is not wiſe*; the other by affirming *he is rich.*

§ 3. ANOTHER Division of Propositions is into such as are *simple* and such as are *compound*.---If a Proposition expresseth but one Judgment of the Mind, and cannot be properly resolved into more Propositions, or the full Sense of it may be expressed in one Proposition in which there is but one Attribute predicated on but one Subject, it is called a *simple Proposition*; as, *God is good:* And these are either *absolute*, when the Predicate is expressive of something essential to the Subject, or directly predicated of it, and no Condition is either expressed or understood, as, *The Sun is bright*; or *conditional*, when there is some Condition annexed to the Subject, upon the Supposition of which, the Predicate is affirmed or denied of it; as, *If God be good, he cannot delight in the Misery of his Creatures.* These conditional Propositions have, by some, been reckoned among the Compounds; but ought not, by the Definition above given, tho' they have that Appearance; they being reducible to one Proposition, as in this Example; it is only as much as to say, *God being good cannot delight in Misery.*---On the contrary, a *compound Proposition* is expressive of several Judgments of the Mind, and may be resolved into two or more Propositions, there being two or more Subjects, or two or more Predicates, connected by Conjunctions; as, *The Sun is bright and round*; *Both Wisdom and Riches are desirable.*---And these *compound Propositions* are either *Copulatives* or *Disjunctives*, according as the Parts are connected by *copulative* or *disjunctive* Conjunctions; as, *Both* Peter *and* Paul *were Apostles and Martyrs.*---*The World exists either of itself, or from a most wise and powerful Cause.*

Of Propositions simple and compound.

§ 4.

Of Propositions True and False.

§ 4. But the most important Distinction of Propositions is, into such as are *True* or *False*.---If we join or separate, *i. e.* affirm or deny Things as being what they really are, the Proposition is *True*; as, *Gold is heavier than Silver*, or *Silver is not so ductile as Gold*.---But if we affirm or deny Things otherwise than they really are, the Proposition is *False*; as, *Money is better than Virtue*, or *Learning is not so good as Riches*.---And here it may be remarked, that the proper original Notion of *Truth* (as was above observed, Chap. II. § 15.) is, that it consists in the *Agreement of any Thing with its Standard*.---GOD's infinite Intellect, comprehending all that is, is the original Standard. He himself is said to be infinite Truth, or the Truth itself, as being infinitely intelligible and perfectly known to his own infinite Intellect, and conformable to it in all that he is and does; and all Things that exist, are what they are originally in his eternal archetypal Idea, or as they are known to him, whether they be Things necessary or contingent.---And the Truth of Things created consists in their Conformity to their Archetype, as they actually exist in Nature and Fact, partaking of so much Truth and Reality as the great Author of them thought fit to assign them. This is, what is called, *Metaphysical Truth*, as above explained.---And now, this *Existence of Things* as they really are, whether in the eternal Mind, if they are *Things necessary*, or in the Nature and Fact, if they are *Things contingent*, must be the Standard to our Minds, and our *Knowledge* or *Judgment* of them is then *Truth*, when we conceive and affirm of them as being what they really are.---This is called *Logical* or *Mental Truth*.

 ---And,

---And, laſtly, our Thoughts and Judgments of Things muſt be the Standard to our Words and Expreſſions concerning them; which are then *Truth*, when they agree with the real Senſe and Apprehenſion of our Minds.---This is called *Verbal Truth*; and when we deſign nothing but to ſpeak as we think, it is called *Moral Truth*.---Since therefore Truth is inflexible, and Things are what they are whatever we think of them, and no Imagination or Opinion of ours can, in the leaſt, alter them; it concerns us above all Things to think and ſpeak of them, as well as to affect and act with regard to them, exactly as being what they really are.

Of Propositions necessary and contingent.

§ 5. As all Things are in their own Nature either *neceſſary* or *contingent* (as was ſhewn above, Chap. II. § 11.) ſo are the Propoſitions expreſſive of them.---Here therefore it is needful to explain this Diſtinction of Propoſitions.---Accordingly, thoſe *Propoſitions* we call *neceſſary*, which aſſert Things or Relations which are in their own Nature neceſſary, immutable and eternal, and which (as was above explained) being founded in the infinite Perfection of the divine Nature, are independent on the divine Will, and therefore cannot be altered by the Power of God himſelf, becauſe it would involve ſome Abſurdity or Contradiction; as, *Some Being muſt have always exiſted*;---*no Being can begin to be without a Cauſe*;---*Triangles of the ſame Baſe and Height are equal*;---*Benefits deſerve Gratitude*, &c.---And thoſe neceſſary Propoſitions, whoſe Evidence is intuitive, are called *Axioms* or *Maxims*. Theſe Truths, with all their neceſſary Conſequences, are, as it were, ſo many Rays of that divine intellectual Light above asserted (Chap. I. § 13. 4. and Chap. II. § 3.) which incessantly flow from the great Fountain of Light, and shine alike into all created Minds.---Of this Kind are a Multitude of *metaphysical*, *mathematical* and *moral* Truths, which, it is evident, must be of a divine Original, since, like the Deity, they are every where present to all Minds, immutable and eternal, and cannot derive from any created Light, or the actual Existence of the Creatures, which is evidently precarious and contingent, tho' they are subservient to lead us up to those Truths that are necessary and eternal.---On the other Hand, those *Propositions* are *contingent*, which assert Things and Relations that are contingent, as depending on the Wills and Powers of free Agents, and consequently might not have been had they so pleased, and the non-existence of them implies no Absurdity, as, *The Sun shines*;---*John runs*.---And of this Kind are all *physical* Truths which relate to created Natures, and which depend on the free arbitrary Will of the Deity, and Matters of meer Institution; and all *political* and *historical* Truths, which depend on the free Exertion of human Wills.

Of Propositions self evident and demonstrable.

§ 6. Now the Truth or Falshood of some Propositions is *self evident*, which we are said to know by *Intuition*; either by *Sense*, as when *I actually perceive Light, Colours*, &c. or by Consciousness and pure Intellect; as, when I say, *I know that I am*, and that *nothing can produce itself*, and that *the Whole is equal to all its Parts*, &c.---The Reason of this intuitive Evidence is, that the Attribute appears at first Sight to be included in the Subject, or connected

nected with it.---But if the Connexion between the Subject and Attribute doth not appear at first Sight, the Terms being duly explained, we must make use of a third Idea or Notion called a *Reason* or *Argument*, which may serve as a common Measure or Standard whereby to judge of the Connexion between them; which, if it evidently appears to agree with each of the Terms of the Proposition, it demonstrates their Agreement between themselves, and if with but one of them, it demonstrates their Disagreement; as, since I know *I began to be, and nothing can begin to be without a Cause*, this demonstratively proves that *I must have had a Cause of my Existence.*--- And as *Knowledge* implies a clear Perception of the Agreement or Disagreement between the Subject and Predicate, we are said in both these Cases to have *Knowledge*, *Certainty* and *Evidence*: In the former, to have *intuitive Certainty*, or *Knowledge by Intuition*; and in the latter to have *demonstrative Certainty*, or *Knowledge by Demonstration*; and the Certainty of *Demonstration* is always ultimately resolved into the Certainty of *Intuition.*---And in all Cases, the *Criterion* or Test of Evidence and Certainty, is, that it is not in our Power to with-hold our Assent or Acquiescence.---This is called *Science*, which Term is however, by some, restrained to those Truths which are necessary and immutable.

Of Propositions doubtful and probable.

§ 7. On the other Hand, we find it, many Times, in our Power, and even that, in some Cases, we are obliged to with-hold our Assent for want of perfect Evidence, or a high Probability, there being some good Reasons to *doubt.*--- Now if the Reasons against the Truth

of

of any Proposition rather preponderate when duly compared with the Reasons for it, it is called *doubtful*.---On the contrary, if the Reasons for it manifestly appear to prevail over those against it, it is said to be *probable*: Thus we say, it is *doubtful*, *whether the Comets are inhabited*, because they seem to be in an irregular chaotic State: But it is *probable* that *the Planets are inhabited*, because they appear to be vast Globes in a settled regular Condition, analogous to our Earth, and no other good End can be assigned them. Yet it is only *probable*, because we do not know enough of them to be perfectly sure that no other good End can be answered by them, and it is possible to be otherwise.---And of these Doubts and Probabilities there are endlessly various Degrees, according to the various Numbers and Weight of the Reasons for or against them; and they also variously appear more or less probable or doubtful to different Persons, according as they have more or less Capacity or Opportunity to examine them, and according as they give their Attention more or less to the Consideration of them. And when any Proposition is supported with all the Reasons it is, in the Nature of it, capable of, and there remains no sufficient Reason to doubt of the Truth of it, we are then said to have a *moral Certainty*, and our Assent to it is called a *Persuasion*, which implies a settled Acquiescence of the Mind in the Truth of it.

Of Opinion and Faith, and Rules of Assent.

§ 8. If the Reasons for the Probability or moral Certainty of any Proposition are taken from the Nature of the Things considered in themselves, our Assent to it is called *Opinion*; as when I say, *I am of Opinion that the Pla-*

nets

nets are inhabited, from the Reaſons that are taken from the Nature of them, ſo far as we can come to the Knowledge of it; which Term alſo is, by ſome, uſed to ſignify our Aſſent to all contingent Propoſitions, however ſo certain.---But if the Reaſons of our Aſſent are taken only or chiefly from the Teſtimony of others (as ſuppoſe we were told by credible Perſons that came from the Planets, that they are inhabited) it is called *Faith*, which will be ſtronger or weaker according to the Credibility of the Thing in itſelf, and the Number and Credibility of the Perſons atteſting it;---who, if they be Men, one or more, it is called *Human Faith*; ſuch as that whereby I believe there is ſuch a Place as *Conſtantinople*, and that there were ſuch Men as *Alexander* and *Julius Cæſar*, &c. And when any Fact of our Times is aſſerted by the concurrent Teſtimony of all Men, or any ancient Fact is atteſted by the univerſal Suffrage of all Antiquity, uninterruptedly handed down to us from Age to Age, we have the higheſt *moral Certainty*, which ſcarce leaves Room for poſſible Doubt.---But if any Propoſition be atteſted by God himſelf, our Aſſent, or Acquieſcence in the Truth of it, is called *divine Faith*, ſuch as that whereby I believe there will be a *Reſurrection*, and a *future Judgment*, &c.--- And this Faith muſt intirely exclude all Doubt, if we are morally ſure that the Propoſition comes from God, and that we rightly underſtand it, becauſe we are demonſtratively certain, that he can neither deceive nor be deceived, ſo that *Faith* is at the Bottom grounded upon *Reaſon*.---And in all Caſes, if the Subject be not capable of clear Evidence, we muſt be content with ſuch Proof as the Nature of it will admit of; having alſo a due Regard

Regard to the Importance of it; and always be determined by the greateſt Probability; and if that cannot be had, and we are obliged to act, we muſt be determined by the greateſt Safety and Advantage.

CHAP. IV.

Of the Mind *reaſoning and methodizing its Thoughts.*---

Of Reaſon in general.

§ 1. NOW, *Thirdly*, that Act of the Mind which ſeeks Reaſons or Arguments to prove the Truth or Falſhood of any Propoſition, and makes uſe of them to that Purpoſe is called Reaſon.---In order to the right Exerciſe of which, it is neceſſary,---*Firſt*, That we carefully conſider the Words of the *Propoſition* to be proved or inquired into, which is now called the *Queſtion*, and all the Words and Terms we make uſe of in our Argumentations upon it; and mark well what Ideas or Conceptions we annex to them, and always uſe the ſame Word in the ſame Senſe, that we may induſtriouſly avoid all Ambiguity.---And, *Secondly*, That we conſider exactly the Ideas or Notions themſelves ſignified by them, as much as poſſible, diveſted of the Words, and recount and conſider the Parts and Properties whereof they conſiſt, that we may ſee how far our intuitive Knowledge goes, *i. e.* what Attributes do, at firſt Sight, appear to be included in the Subject, or related to it, and what kind of Relation they bear; that, by this Means, carefully ſifting and canvaſſing the Matter, and ſeparating

rating what is clear from what is doubtful, we may first be sure where the Doubt lies, and wherein the Merits of the Cause do really consist.

§ 2. THESE Things being first duly observed, the right Exercise of Reason properly consists,---*First*, In taking a careful Survey of all the Relations which the Subject or Predicate of the Question, or disputed Proposition, bear to any other Ideas or Notions, and thereby searching out and discovering some third Idea or Conception related to one or other, or both of them, which is called the Reason or Argument, and, as I said, may be considered as a common Measure by which to judge of the Relation between them; the Foundation of which is that grand Maxim above mentioned (Chap. II. § 22.) That *those Things which agree or differ in a Third, must agree or differ between themselves*; this is called *Sagacity*.---To which Purpose it is necessary that we endeavour to consider the Whole of Things, and as far as we can, make ourselves Masters of our Subject; and in many Cases it may be of good Use to have Recourse to the several Topicks above explained in the second Chapter, Causes, Effects, *&c*.---And as all our Reasoning takes its Rise from self-evident Propositions, we must see to it, that the Connexion between them and those we would prove, be made as clear and evident as possible before we proceed to a Conclusion. And, *Secondly*, When we have found an Argument, and duly considered its Relation to the Terms of the Question, the Act of Reason consists in inferring, from the Agreement or Disagreement of the Subject and Attribute of the Question with this intermediate Idea or Conception, their Agreement or

Of the right Exercise of Reason.

Repug-

Repugnancy between themſelves: This is called *Illation.*---Thus, ſuppoſe the Queſtion were, *Whether Virtue be more valuable than Riches?*---I firſt conſider the Nature of *Virtue* and *Riches* in all their Properties and Relations; I compare them with each other, and particularly with regard to our *Happineſs*, which alone can render any Thing more or leſs valuable to us; and then, from that general ſelf-evident Propoſition, That, *what moſt contributes to our Happineſs is moſt valuable*, I infer, That, *ſince Virtue conduceth vaſtly more to our Happineſs than Riches*, it muſt upon that Account, *be vaſtly more valuable.*

Of the Nature of Syllogiſm.

§ 3. The Method of Reaſoning in the Schools is called *Syllogiſm*, which conſiſts in comparing the intermediate Idea or Argument, *Firſt*, With the *Predicate* of the Queſtion, which is called the *Major Term*, as being generally the moſt extenſive; for which Reaſon the firſt Propoſition is called the *Major*; *Secondly*, With the Subject of it, which is called the *Minor Term*, and therefore this ſecond Propoſition is called the *Minor*, and theſe two are called the Premiſes: And then, *Thirdly*, In making the Concluſion according as it is found to agree or diſagree with both, or either of them. If it is found to agree with both, it is affirmative; if with but one, it is negative.---As, ſuppoſe the Queſtion were, *Whether Juſtice ought always to be practiſed?*---The Argument ſhall be the *Advantageouſneſs* of it.---Then the *Major* Propoſition will be, *What is advantageous in the whole is always to be practiſed:* The *Minor*, That *Juſtice is ever advantageous in the whole:*---Then the *Concluſion* will be, That *Juſtice is always to be practiſed.*---Or, *what is miſchievous to Society ought not to be practiſed*; *Lying is miſchievous to Society*;

ciety ;---therefore *Lying ought not to be practiſed.* ---The Ground of which Method of Reaſoning is this Maxim: That *whatever can truly be univerſally affirmed or denied of any Subject, may truly be affirmed or denied of all or any of the Particulars or Individuals comprehended under that Subject.*---And if either of the Premiſes be yet doubtful, being denied, it muſt be proved after the ſame Manner as before, till we arrive at two Premiſes, neither of which can reaſonably admit of any Doubt.

§ 4. *Of the three Figures of Categorick Syllogiſms.*

SYLLOGISMS of this Kind are called the *Categorick* Forms, as being expreſſed abſolutely, and always conſiſt of only ſimple Propoſitions.---In which the moſt uſual and uſeful are thoſe, wherein the intermediate Idea or Argument precedes, as being the Subject in the Major Propoſition, which is always univerſal and follows, being the Predicate in the Minor, which is always affirmative; and this is called the *firſt Figure*: As, *An infinitely wiſe and good Being cannot delight in the Miſery of his Creatures:--- God is an infinitely wiſe and good Being* ;---therefore, *God cannot delight in the Miſery of his Creatures.* But in ſome Caſes it may be moſt convenient to make the middle Term the Predicate of both the Premiſes, one of which is always negative, and the Major univerſal; this is called the *ſecond Figure*, as *All Virtue is amiable*; *Avarice is not amiable*; therefore, *Avarice is not a Virtue.* And laſtly, ſometimes it may be moſt convenient to make the middle Term the Subject of both the Premiſes; which is called the third Figure; in which the Minor muſt be affirmative, and the Concluſion is always particular; as, Solomon *did not*

not always act wisely: But Solomon *was a wise Man*; therefore, *some wise Man doth not always act wisely*, or, which is the same, *All wise Men do not always act wisely.* Much is here said by Logicians of the *Modes* of Syllogisms under each of these Figures, which is rather Matter of Curiosity than Use; but if any one desires to gratify his Curiosity, he may see a most complete and accurate Account of them in the *Port-Royal Art of Thinking.*

Of the Hypothetick Syllogism.

§ 5. BUT the same Arguments may be disposed more familiarly in what is called the *Hypothetick Form*, the *Major* of which is a conditional Proposition, as in the former Example: *If virtue is, in the whole, more conducive to our Happiness than Riches, it is more valuable: But it is in the whole more conducive to our Happiness: Therefore it is more valuable.* So in a later Instance: *If Lying be mischievous to Society, it ought not to be practised: But it is mischievous,* &c. *therefore ought not to be practised.* Here the major Proposition consists of two Parts, which are called the Antecedent and the Consequent, and the Argument proceeds from the affirming or Position of the Antecedent to the Position of the Consequent. But there is another Form of it which proceeds from taking away of the Consequent to taking away of the Antecedent, as, *If I had said such a Thing, I should have thought of it*; *But I never thought of it, therefore I never said it.*

Of the Disjunctive Syllogism.

§ 6. THERE is likewise another Form of Syllogism which is called the *Disjunctive Form*, in which the Parts must be Opposites, so that the Position of the first must infer the taking away of the

the other, or of all the reſt, if there be more than two; or the taking away of the latter, or all the reſt, if more than two, muſt infer the Poſition of the former; as, *Every Man ſerves either God or Mammon:* Peter *ſerves God, therefore he cannot ſerve Mammon:* or, Judas *ſerves Mammon, therefore cannot be a Servant of God.* And to give an Inſtance where there are more than two, *Every Action is either good, bad or indifferent; but to relieve a poor Man is a good Action;* therefore it is *neither bad nor indifferent*; or, it is *neither bad nor indifferent*; therefore *it is a good Action.*

Of irregular Syllogiſms.

§ 7. These are the chief Forms of Reaſoning to which all others, that are of any Conſequence, may be reduced. It may not however be amiſs to ſay ſomething of thoſe which are called *irregular Syllogiſms.* Of which, ſome are *redundant*, as conſiſting of more than three Propoſitions, of which Number only regular Syllogiſms conſiſt: In which Caſe, a Reaſon is added to ſupport either the Major or Minor, or both, before we proceed to the Concluſion. Others are *deficient*, as when the *Major* is left out or ſuppreſſed in the Mind, being underſtood, tho' not expreſſed; as, *Virtue conduces more to our Happineſs than Riches, therefore it is more excellent*; ſuch are called *Enthymems.* But the moſt noted of theſe irregular Syllogiſms are the *Dilemma* and the *Sorites.* In a *Dilemma*, the major Propoſition is a Conditional, whoſe Conſequent contains all the ſeveral Suppoſitions upon which the Antecedent can take Place, which being removed in the Minor, it is apparent the Antecedent muſt alſo be taken away; as, *If God did not create the World, it muſt either have been*

ſelf-

ſelf-exiſtent, or have derived from meer Chance; but it could neither be ſelf-exiſtent nor derive from Chance; therefore it muſt have been created by God. Sorites is a Method of arguing in a Series of Propoſitions, ſo connected together, that the Predicate of the firſt becomes the Subject of the ſecond, and ſo on, till we come to a Concluſion, in which the Predicate of the laſt Propoſition appears from thoſe intermediate Propoſitions to be connected with the Subject of the firſt. For an Example of the *Sorites*, we may ſet down the following Way of Reaſoning, to prove the natural Immortality of the Soul.

1. The Soul is a conſcious, intelligent, active, ſelf-exerting Being.

2. A conſcious, intelligent, active, ſelf-exerting Being, as ſuch, is intirely of an oppoſite and different Nature and Kind from that of Bodies, and therefore can have nothing common with them but bare Exiſtence.

3. A Being that, as ſuch, is intirely of a different Nature from Bodies, and hath nothing beſides Exiſtence common with them, can have no corporeal Properties and Affections, ſuch as ſolid Extenſion, Continuity of Parts, and Diviſibility or Diſcerpibility.

4. A Being that, having no corporeal Properties, and ſo does not conſiſt of ſolid extended Parts, diviſible or diſcerpible, cannot be naturally liable to a Diſſolution.

5. What is not, in the Nature of it, liable to a Diſſolution, muſt be naturally immortal. *Ergo*,

6. The Soul is naturally immortal. And here theſe intermediate Propoſitions may be reduced to ſo many categorick Syllogiſms, beginning with the laſt, and ending with the firſt.

§ 8. THOUGH the Rules given above, if duly attended to, would effectually prevent all sophistical Reasoning; yet it may not be amiss to add a few Words concerning what are called *Sophisms* or false Reasonings; among which, the chief are, 1. That which is called *Ignoratio Elenchi*, which is, when the Dispute proceeds upon a Mistake, occasioned by not attending to the true Meaning or State of the Question. 2. *Petitio principii*, which is, when in pretending to argue, the Thing is taken for granted which was to be proved; this we call Begging the Question. 3. *Fallacia quatuor terminorum*, which is, when the intermediate Term bears a different Sense in the Minor, from the Sense in which it was used in the Major. 4. *Non Causa pro Causa*, which is, when that is, by Mistake, taken for a Cause, which was not the Cause; as, when a Person receives his Health consequent to the using such a Medicine, and ascribes it to that, when perhaps it might really be owing to a Medicine which he had used before. And 5thly, the last I shall mention, is that which ariseth from what is called the *Association of Ideas*, where because such Ideas are connected meerly by Custom, we are apt to conceit they are connected in Nature, as Terrors with Darkness. On which Account it is of great Importance in Education, to take Care that no Ideas become associated by Habit or Custom but those that are connected in Nature; and on the other Hand, that those Ideas that are really connected in Nature be associated by Habit or Custom, that a Sense of their Connection may operate with the greater Force in the Conduct of Life. And thus much for *Syllogism*.

Of Sophisms.

§ 9. THE

§ 9. THE laſt Thing in Logick, is that Courſe of Reaſoning which is called *Method*, which is only a regular Proceeding in connecting a large Series of Reaſonings or Inſtructions on any Subject, and therefore truly belongs to this Part of Logick which treats of Reaſoning. For in delineating a whole Science, or treating on any large Subject, it is neceſſary to purſue it thro' a long Chain of Reaſoning, or a whole Series of Propoſitions mutually related; in which it is of great Importance, both for the clearer underſtanding it, and the better remembering it, that we carefully obſerve the Order that Nature itſelf points out to us; ſo as to begin with what is plain and ſimple, and thence to proceed gradually to what is more compounded and obſcure; ſo ordering and ranging Things through the whole Proceſs, that what goes before may continually reflect Light upon what is to follow, and pave the Way to it; and taking the utmoſt Care to preſerve Evidence, or at leaſt the higheſt poſſible Degree of Probability in every Step, till we arrive at the higheſt Truth and Good, or the Concluſion we aim at.---In order to which, the beſt Thing we can do, is to obſerve diligently the Manner in which the beſt Writers proceed, in treating on any Subject they propoſe to handle, and particularly, the Mathematicians, and Moraliſts.---Now, I ſay, ſuch a Series of Reaſonings we call *Method*; which, if it begin with Effects, and ariſeth to the Diſcovery of Cauſes, or with particular Facts, Parts or Properties, and ariſeth gradually to the Whole, and to general Principles, and Concluſions, it is called the *Analytical Method*.---But if it begin with Cauſes already diſcovered, and deſcend to

Of Method.

Effects, or with general Principles, and descend, by the Application of them, to the Illustration or Proof of Particulars or Facts, it is called the *Synthetical Method*.---The first is used in searching and discovering Truth; the second chiefly in teaching it in the most compendious Manner, when it is discovered.

Of the disinterested Love of Truth.

§ 10. But in order to succeed well in the right Use of our Reason, be the Form or Method what it will, whether in Thinking or Reasoning by ourselves, or in a joint Searching after Truth, in our Conversation with others, which should be our only View in what is called Disputation, it is of the greatest Importance that we observe some such Rules as these; 1. That we habitually consider the Knowledge of *Truth*, as being the highest Perfection and Happiness of our Minds, which therefore should be our grand Pursuit, separate from every other Consideration. 2. That accordingly we possess ourselves of an ardent and disinterested Love of Truth, for its own intrinsic Excellency; and of the utmost Aversion to all Falshood and Deceit, or being any ways misled or imposed upon by false Colours, and delusive Appearances. 3. That in order to this, we honestly endeavour as much as possible to divest ourselves of all sinister Views and Prejudices, in favour of any vulgar Opinions, pre-conceived Schemes, or worldly Interests, and guard ourselves against every untoward Appetite or Passion, that may darken or byass our Minds, and so keep them as calm as possible, and open and ready to the Impressions of the naked Truth. 4. In order the better to come at Truth, we must endeavour to consider, with the utmost Attention,

Attention, the Things themselves, with all their various Relations and Connections, divested of the Delusions and Ambiguities of Words, which are many times apt to mislead us. 5. And lastly, we must enlarge our Views as much as possible, so as to take the Whole of Things into our Consideration, without which we cannot make any tolerable Judgment of what relates to Particulars. If we would faithfully observe these and the like Rules for the Conduct of our Understandings, and at the same time, be, above all Things, concerned to do our Duty, and to know the Truth, with this honest View, to be governed by it in Heart and Life, with all Humility, and *without Partiality or Hypocrisy*, we should not be in Danger of being misled into any great or dangerous Mistakes, but should attain to know the Truth, *and the Truth would make us free.*---And thus much for the several Objects and Operations of the Understanding, which are the Subject of *Logicks.*

CHAP. V.

Of the Mind *affecting*, *willing* and *acting*.

Of the Passions in general.

§ 1. HAVING thus given some Account of the Subject of *Logicks*, which relate to the Conduct of the Intellect, in its various Exertions, I now go on to give a short Sketch of the Subject of *Ethics*, which relate to the Conduct of our Affections and Behaviour; of which no more is here intended, than what is just necessary, in order to the Business of the next Chapter.---Here therefore,

fore, according to what was obſerved above (Chap. I. § 12.) we are to treat, 1. Of our *affecting* or *diſaffecting* Things, according as they appear good or bad. 2. Of our *chuſing* or *refuſing*, willing, or nilling them, according as we affect or diſaffect them. And, 3. Of our freely *acting*, or *forbearing* to act, according to the Judgment and Choice we have made. *Firſt* then, we are to conſider the *Affections* or *Paſſions*, of which we are conſcious, and which next occur to be obſerved in the Frame of our rational Nature, the Doctrine or Explication of which is called *Pathology*; for no ſooner doth any Object come under the Mind's Conſideration, but it appears agreeable or diſagreeable, according as it is, by the eſtabliſhed Law of our Nature, attended with Pleaſure or Pain, or, at leaſt, with ſome Degree of Satisfaction or Uneaſineſs, or the Apprehenſion of it.---Now, by the *Paſſions*, we mean in general, ſuch Affections or Diſaffections, Inclinations or Averſions, as we experience in ourſelves, upon feeling or expecting that Pleaſure or Uneaſineſs with which any Object is attended.---And ſuch is the Law of Union between our Souls and Bodies, that upon our being affected or diſaffected towards any Object, we are ſenſible of certain Commotions and Perturbations in our Blood and Spirits, correſponding and in Proportion to thoſe pleaſing or diſpleaſing Apprehenſions.

Of the Paſſions more particularly.

§ 2. Now the leading Paſſion, and which ſeems in ſome Degree to be at the Bottom in all our Paſſions, is what we call *Admiration* or *Wonder*, which, in a high Degree, is called *Aſtoniſhment*, and is that Sentiment which we feel on the Perception of any Thing that is new, or or great, or what we are unaccuſtomed to, or from which we have ſtrong Apprehenſions of Pleaſure or Uneaſineſs.---And more particularly, when we are delighted in any Thing, as being attended with Pleaſure, we are ſaid to *love* it; and if we actually poſſeſs the Pleaſure, it is attended with *Joy*.---If the Object of our Affection be a Perſon, our Love may be called *Eſteem*; and if the Perſon be in Miſery, it is called *Pity* or *Compaſſion*: And if the Object be abſent or future, it hath the Name of *Deſire* or *Hope*.---On the other Hand, when we are diſaffected towards any Object, apprehending it to be attended with Pain or Uneaſineſs, we are ſaid to *hate* it; and the actual Sufferance of that Pain or Uneaſineſs is called *Grief*; and *Shame*, if it ariſe from the Conſciouſneſs of our own Miſconduct; and if the Object be a mean and deſpicable Character, the Paſſion is called *Contempt*; and if the Evil be future and impending, it is Terror, or *Fear*.---If the Object from which we feel or apprehend Pleaſure, be procured, or occur to us by Means of any Perſon or free Agent, deſigning Good to us, we call our Sentiment on that Occaſion, *Benevolence*, *Complacence* and *Gratitude*, attended with a Deſire to reward it; and with Joy at any Good, or Grief at any Ill that occurs to our Friend or Benefactor: And this Temper, if it ariſe to a ſettled Habit of mutual Good-will and good Offices, we call *Friendſhip*. But, on the other Hand, if the Object from whence we feel or apprehend Pain or Uneaſineſs be procured or occur to us by Means of any free Agent, deſigning any Evil or Miſchief to us, we call our Sentiment on that Occaſion, *Malevolence*, *Anger*, or *Reſentment*, which is apt to be attended with a

Desire to revenge it; and with Joy at any Evil that befals our Enemy, or Grief at any Good that may occur to him, which is called *Envy*. And if this Temper groweth to a settled Habit of Ill-will towards the supposed injurious Person, it acquireth the Name of *Malice*.

Of the End and Use of them.

§ 3. THESE *Passions* are natural to us, and, as such, must be considered as Part of the Frame of our Natures, and consequently as being implanted in us by the Author of our Nature, for answering very wise and good Ends, relating to our Happiness; and therefore are so far from being evil in themselves, that they have the Nature of Good, as well as all our other Faculties, and so, like the rest, become morally Good or Evil, according to the good or ill Use we make of them. Now as God hath so framed us, that our Happiness should depend on a vigorous Activity in the Use of the Powers and Faculties he hath given us, his Design in planting these Passions in us, was, that they might be, as it were, Spurs and Incentives in us, to put us upon such a vigorous Activity, in avoiding those Things that are mischievous either to ourselves or others, and pursuing those Things in which our Happiness or that of others consists. For the Passions are, as it were, the Wings of the Soul, by which it is carried on with Vehemence and Impetuosity in its several Pursuits; and, as it were, its Springs, by which it is animated and invigorated in all its Exertions. Thus *Love*, *Desire* and *Hope*, vigorously animate and spur us on to the Pursuit of those Things that we love, desire and hope for, as being connected with our Well-being and Happiness; and *Hatred*, *Abhorrence* and *Fear*, engage

engage us with the utmoſt Vehemence to fly from, and guard againſt, thoſe Things that we abhor and dread, as tending to our Miſery. And as *Benevolence*, *Compaſſion* and *Gratitude*, inſpire us with a Delight in all thoſe good Offices in which both our perſonal and ſocial Happineſs conſiſts; ſo *Malevolence*, *Averſion* and *Anger*, are uſeful to inſpire us with Indignation and Zeal, in oppoſing all thoſe impious and injurious Practices that tend to the Miſchief and Miſery of Society in general, as well as each particular Perſon.

Of the due Government of them.

§ 4. So that the *Paſſions* are deſigned to be, and are, in their Nature, capable of being ſubſervient to a Multitude of excellent Purpoſes; and all that is neceſſary to render them ſo, is, that there be a right Judgment made, what Objects we ought to affect or diſaffect, as being really connected with our Happineſs or Miſery, either perſonal or ſocial; and that they be duly ballanced one with another, and rightly governed and moderated in Proportion to the real Value and Importance of their reſpective Objects. And for this Purpoſe were we furniſhed with the Powers of *Reaſon* and *Conſcience*, that they might preſide over our Paſſions, and make a right Judgment of their ſeveral Objects, and thence preſcribe Laws to them, and reſtrain them from all Exorbitancies and Irregularities; that we might know what we ought to *love* or *hate*, to *hope* for or *fear*, to be *pleaſed* or *diſpleaſed* with, and in what Proportion, and not to ſuffer them to exceed the real Value and Importance of Things with regard to our true Happineſs. Since, therefore, the great Author of our Nature aims at our Happineſs, and hath given us our Paſſions

to

to be subservient to it, and furnished us with Reason, to govern and regulate them in such a Manner as to render them useful to that End, it must be his Will and Law, and the Law of our Nature, that we should duly exercise our Reason in the right Government of them, so as not to suffer them to hurry us on into such Actions as our Reason and Conscience disallow, as being contrary to the eternal Laws of Justice and Benevolence: And one of the chief Concerns in Culture and Education is, to discipline and moderate the Passions, and to inure them to a ready Submission to the Dictates of Reason and Conscience.

Of Will, Activity and Liberty.

§ 5. AND *lastly*, in consequence of any Object's appearing agreeable or disagreeable to our Minds, as tending to our Pleasure or Uneasiness, and being accordingly affected or disaffected, the last Things I mentioned, of which we are conscious in ourselves, and which I shall here briefly take together, are the Powers of *chusing* the one, and *refusing* the other, and our *Wills* to act, or not to act, with a Power of *free Activity*, whereby we are able spontaneously to exert ourselves for obtaining the one, and avoiding the other. Now, as our true Happiness consists in being secure from all Pain or Uneasiness, which is called *natural Evil*, and in being possessed of such Pleasures and Satisfactions as are suitable to our Nature in the Whole of it, which are called *natural Good*; so our highest *natural Perfection* consists in being capable of rightly judging and chusing for ourselves, and of a free and vigorous Activity, conformable to our best Judgment and Choice, for avoiding the one, and attaining the other.

other. And as our *Reaſon* was plainly given us, to enable us to make a right Judgment what we ought to chuſe and avoid, and to do and forbear, in order to our true Happineſs, in the Whole of our Nature and Duration; and our *Will* conſiſts in freely reſolving and determining ourſelves to the one or the other, as they ſhall appear to our Judgment; ſo our higheſt *moral Perfection* conſiſts in actually making a right Judgment, what we ought to affect or diſaffect, and to do and forbear; and in *freely* and habitually exerting ourſelves in chuſing and doing the one, and rejecting and forbearing the other, conformable thereunto. I ſay *freely*; for Freedom or *Liberty* conſiſteth in having a Power to act, or not to act, as we pleaſe, and conſequently to ſuſpend judging or acting, till we have taken Opportunity to make as deliberate and exact a Judgment as ever we can, what is beſt for us in the Whole, to do or forbear; as *Neceſſity*, on the other Hand, conſidered as oppoſed to Liberty, implieth, that it is out of our Power to ſuſpend acting, or to do otherwiſe than we do, in which Caſe there can be neither Praiſe nor Blame.

Of the right governing our Activity & our higheſt moral Perfection.

§ 6. I SAY our higheſt *moral Perfection* conſiſts in freely doing what we know tends to make us intirely happy in the Whole of our Nature and Duration: But then it muſt be conſidered, that, as GOD is our chief Good, our great Creator, Preſerver and Governor, on whom we do intirely depend for our Being, and for all our Happineſs, and all our Hopes; and as he wills our Happineſs, as his End in giving and continuing our Beings, and conſequently every Thing as a Means, that

is

is conducive to it; ſo it muſt be ſuppoſed to be implied in our higheſt moral Perfection, that we be intirely devoted to Him, and do every Thing conducive to our Happineſs, in Relation to *Him*, *ourſelves*, and *one another*, in a deſigned Conformity to Him as our great Original and Pattern, and in Compliance with his Will, and from a Senſe of Duty to Him as our ſupreme moral Governor. And conſequently, that, as by Reaſon of our great Ignorance and Weakneſs, we ſtand in much Need of his Inſtruction and Aſſiſtance, in order to judge what is truly conducive to our Happineſs, and to put it in Practice; it muſt imply a moſt grateful and ready Submiſſion to his Inſtructions and Injunctions, and Dependance upon his Aids and Aſſiſtances to render all our Endeavours ſucceſsful, in the Purſuit of our true and everlaſting Happineſs. But the more particular Proſecution of theſe Subjects will be the Buſineſs of *Ethics* or *Moral Philoſophy*, eſpecially as it is improved by *Chriſtianity*.

CHAP. VI.

Of the *Progreſs of the Mind, from its firſt Notices, towards its utmoſt Perfection.*

Of the Mind's Progreſs, from its firſt Notices.

§ 1. MEAN time, I would, in Purſuance of my firſt Deſign, make a few Obſervations, agreeable to the Sketch here laid down, on the gradual Progreſs of the human Mind, from the firſt Notices of *Senſe* and *Intellect*, to its higheſt Perfection and Happineſs. And as to its firſt Notices, they are doubtleſs thoſe of *Senſe*, but directly joined

joined with a *Conſciouſneſs* of its Perceptions.--- Warmth and Hunger, and probably ſome Pains, are, perhaps, all the Senſations it hath before its Birth; and when it comes into the Light of this World, it is directly impreſſed with the Senſe of Light and Colours, as well as Sounds, Taſtes, Odours, and frequent uneaſy and painful Senſations, *&c.* all which ſtill more and more awaken its Conſciouſneſs; and every freſh Notice of Senſe and Conſciouſneſs, ſtill goes on to excite its Admiration, and engage its Attention. And being a perfect Stranger to every Thing about it, it hath every Thing to learn; to which it diligently applies itſelf, as its Conſciouſneſs more and more awakens, upon the Repetition, every Moment, of freſh Impreſſions of Senſe; till, by Degrees, having a great Number of Feelings, Taſtes, Odours, Sounds, and viſible Objects, frequently repeating their ſeveral Impreſſions, its conſcious Memory ſtill enlarging, it begins, by Means of the intellectual Light, with which it finds its Conſciouſneſs attended, gradually to collect and recollect the ſeveral Relations and Connections it obſerves to obtain among its various Ideas: And at length, when it is in Eaſe, it diſcovereth a wonderful Curioſity and Delight in obſerving theſe Connections, as well as being impreſſed with new Ideas.

Of its Learning Connexions and Languages.

§ 2. It hath been made very evident both by Reaſoning and Experiment, * " That the Objects of Sight and Touch are intirely different and diſtinct Things; that there is no neceſſary Connection between them; that Things viſible are only arbitrary Signs of Things tangible; that

* By Biſhop *Berkley* in his *Theory of Viſion*; and *Philoſophical Tranſactions*, No. 402.

that the one hath the Nature of a Language with Regard to the other, and that the Connection between them is to be learned only by Experience, as that between Words and the Things signified by them:" And particularly, that as all visible Objects or Ideas are only in the Mind; so a Man born blind, and made to see, which must also be the Case of Infants, can have at first no Notion of Distance, nor of any Connection between Things visible and tangible, and consequently, that both Distance and that Connection must be learn'd by long Trial and Experience. It must, therefore, be a Matter of great Exercise of Thought in an infant Mind to learn this Connection, and particularly, to learn the Notion of the various Distances and Situations of Things tangible, by its Observations on the various Degrees of Strength or Weakness, of Vividness or Faintness of the Light reflected from them, in the Things visible constantly connected with them. And, at the same time that it hath these Things to learn, which must be a laborious Work, as being the same Thing with learning a Language, it is also learning the Names of Things, and the Connection and Use of Words, which is another Language. And, as if all these were not Task enough, it hath all this While, to be learning how to use its Limbs; its Hands in handling, its Tongue, and other Organs of Speech, in making and imitating Sounds, and its whole Body in all its Exertions, and particularly, at length, the Poize of its Center of Gravity, and the Use of its Feet in walking.

§ 3. All these Things require a great deal of earnest Application, and the Exercise of much Thought and Experience: So that it seems evident

dent that thoſe little Creatures, from the Beginning, do conſider, reflect and think a prodigious deal more than we are commonly apt to imagine; and I do not ſee how we can avoid admitting that the Soul's Capacity is as great from the firſt Moment as ever it is. For it is plain, from what hath been ſaid, that they learn two diſtinct Languages within the two firſt Years of their Life to a good Degree of Perfection; I mean the Connection between tangible and viſible Objects, and between both of them and Words, and beſides this, a conſiderable Degree of Dexterity in the Uſe of their Limbs, which is, doubtleſs, a great deal more than they ever learn in ſo much Time afterwards. And conſequently the Reaſon why there appear ſo many little, low, weak and childiſh Things in them, which we are apt to deſpiſe and think them beneath our Notice, is not for want of good Senſe and Capacity, but meerly for want of Experience and Opportunity for intellectual Improvements. Hence alſo it appears, that we ought to think little Children to be Perſons of much more Importance than we uſually apprehend them to be; and how indulgent we ſhould be to their inquiſitive Curioſity as being Strangers; with how much Candour, Patience and Care, we ought to bear with them and inſtruct them; with how much Decency, Honour and Integrity, we ought to treat them; and how careful it concerns us to be, not to ſay or do any Thing to them, or before them, that ſavours of Falſhood or Deceit, or that is in any Kind indecent or vitious. *Pueris maxima debetur Reverentia*, is a good trite old Saying.

Of the Capacity of Children, and the Regard due to them.

§ 4. FOR

§ 4. For it is to be observed, in the next Place, that while Children are acquiring a general Knowledge of the sensible World about them, they are at the same time learning the Knowledge of the Persons with whom they converse; their Dependence on them, and the Relations they stand in to them; and a Notion of *meum* and *tuum*, and thence a very quick Sense of Justice and Injury, as well as of good Usage, Benevolence and Gratitude; all which appear obvious to them from Consciousness and Reflection, and Attention to that inward, intuitive, intellectual Light, which as I have observed (Chap. I. § 13. 14.) perpetually shines in upon their little Minds, from the DEITY, *the Father of Lights*, and *the Father of their Spirits*. Hence they soon apprehend the Relations of *Causes* and *Effects*, of *Whole* and *Parts*, of Things *equal*, *greater* or *less*, of Things *like* and *unlike*, of the *same* and Things *different* and *contrary*, of *general Names* and *Notions*, and Analogies from Things sensible to Things spiritual and moral, of Actions *necessary* and *voluntary*, and of Things done with *Design* and by *Accident*, &c. And by Reflection and Observation they judge of others by themselves: So that in three or four Years, they do, with a litttle Teaching, begin to have a Notion of Persons, as being an intirely different and distinct Sort of Beings from meer Objects of Sense. They soon know that a Stone in falling, the Water in running, the Wind in blowing, and the Fire in burning, &c. knows not what it does, and neither acts voluntarily, nor with Design: Whereas a Man or a Boy, they apprehend, if he does what is either pleasing or displeasing, beneficial or

Of their Knowledge of Persons, Relations and Duties.

or injurious to them, he knows what he does, and designs to do it, and might, if he would, do otherwise. From whence, as I said, they have a quick Sense of good or ill Usage, and consequently, of Right and Wrong, and of Gratitude or Resentment, according as they take themselves to be well, or ill treated.

Of their Notions of Praise and Blame, Shame and Guilt, &c.

§ 5. HENCE, with regard to what they do themselves, they, by Reflection, soon acquire the Notions of Free-Agency, and of *Praise* or *Blame*, according as they are conscious of their doing well or ill; *i. e.* according as they are sensible they act a fit and a reasonable Part on the one Hand, or an unreasonable and injurious Part on the other. Thence they soon learn to have a Sense of *Shame* and *Guilt* upon their Consciousness of having done amiss, and of *Satisfaction* and *Self-applause*, when they think they have done well. And hence they quickly learn the Notions of *Law*, *Conscience*, *Sin* and *Duty*, especially if they have had the Rules explained, and been duly chastized or applauded when they have done ill or well, by those on whom they know they have a Dependance, and to whom they find themselves accountable; and to whom to account, as being both their Benefactors and Governors, they are conscious it is fit and reasonable, as they know they stand in much Need of their Help and Conduct in order to their own Well-being. All these Things are obvious in Children of four, five and six Years old, and manifestly derive from that intellectual Light, of which I have often been speaking: And the great Concern of Culture, and a right Education, is to awaken their Attention to this inward intuitive Senſe of True and Falſe, Good and Bad, Right and Wrong; and to fix their Attachment to the one, and their Averſion to the other, by ſteadily affecting them with Applauſe or Blame, Pleaſure or Pain, Joy or Grief, according as they affect or do the one or the other.

How they ſhould be treated, & taught the Notion of the Deity, and their Duty to him.

§ 6. And as the Intellect and Reaſon of Children thus manifeſtly appears to dawn and improve, it ought to be continually *encouraged* and *aſſiſted* by thoſe that are about them, and eſpecially thoſe that have the Conduct of them. As they are got into a World wherein every Thing is new and ſtrange to them, and for want of Knowledge and Experience, they are liable to many Miſtakes in their Apprehenſions, and to make a thouſand Blunders in their Actions and Conduct; and yet in their original Simplicity and Well-meaning, are ordinarily very inquiſitive, and willing to be taught and conducted; it is mightily incumbent on thoſe to whoſe Care they are by Providence committed, whether Parents, Nurſes, Guardians, Maſters or Tutors, to conſider them, with great Candor, as Strangers that need to be conducted and aſſiſted; to be ready to anſwer their little Queſtions, and to teach them to reaſon by candidly reaſoning with them; and to apply themſelves with great Tenderneſs, Patience and Aſſiduity, to guide and inſtruct them. And as they grow capable of conſidering the Connections of *Cauſes* and *Effects*, &c. they ſhould open their Minds, and turn their Attention to the Survey of all Nature, and lead them to obſerve the Contrivance, Beauty and Uſefulneſs of every Thing

Thing before their Eyes, and eſpecially thoſe Things they find moſt neceſſary, uſeful and pleaſing to themſelves, and on which their own Subſiſtance and Comfort more immediately depend; and thence conduct them to the Apprehenſion, and ſome juſt Conceptions, of the true *Cauſe* of every Thing in all Nature, who is truly their *Father* and *Author*, and *upholdeth their Souls in Life, and repleniſheth them with his Loving Kindneſs and tender Mercies*; and who is the great common Father and Lord of all Things, both in Heaven and Earth: And from theſe Apprehenſions, it will be eaſy to teach them to deduce their Duty and Obligations to Him, of Love, Gratitude, Truſt, Reſignation and Obedience, and to be as like Him as ever they are able, *pure as He is pure*, *righteous as He is righteous*, and *kind and merciful as He is*; and to praiſe Him daily for every Thing they enjoy, and pray to Him for whatſoever they want, and to live under an habitual Senſe of their Dependance upon Him, and Obligations to His infinite Goodneſs: To which Purpoſes, let them not only be taught to live in the daily Exerciſe of Devotion by themſelves, but alſo ſteadily attend on the publick Worſhip, both in the Family, and at the Church, where the Sight and Example of others, will mightily contribute to awaken and keep alive in their Minds a Senſe of theſe Things, which will be apt ſtrongly to influence the Conduct of their whole Lives.

Of moral & political Connections and Duties.

§ 7. AND as they begin to grow acquainted with the Family and Neighbourhood, and their Connections with theſe and thoſe that are about them, and to ſee how their own Comfort and Well-being depends on the Eſteem, Love and good Offices of others, and that theſe depend on their own good Conduct, and good Offices towards them; they ſhould have it inculcated upon them, that as they would be ſecure from all Injuries, and the ill Treatment of others, ſo they muſt avoid every Thing that is injurious and abuſive towards them; and as they would expect the Benevolence and good Offices of others, they muſt be full of Good-will, and ready to every good Office towards them; and conſequently, delight in every honeſt, faithful, kind and obliging Thing, whereby they may recommend themſelves to the Confidence, Eſteem and Good-will of all Mankind with whom they have to do. And as they go on to enlarge their Acquaintance with the World about them, and to have a Notion of their Connections with the Town in which they live, and the Government and Kingdom to which they belong, and, in general, with the whole Species; they ſhould be led on to a Senſe of Order and publick Virtue, and the Love of their Country, and finally of the whole human Kind, and to look for their own Weal in that of the whole Community, and even of the whole moral Syſtem, and to a Conduct correſponding thereunto.

Of moderating their Appetites & Paſſions.

§ 8. AND, as from their early Acquaintance with the Objects of their *Appetites*, from whence they derive a very exquiſite Pleaſure, they contract a violent Attachment to them, and an Impatience of whatever may interrupt or controul their Gratification; and as this Impetuoſity is, in many Inſtances, utterly inconſiſtent with their Duty and true Intereſt, both with

with regard to God and Man, and a ſtrong Temptation to the Violation of it; they ſhould, from the Beginning, be taught and inured to the Practice of Self-denial, and the Moderation and Reſtraint of their Appetites and Paſſions, and, as far as they are capable, be ſhewn the Reaſonableneſs and Neceſſity of their ſo doing, in order to their own trueſt Intereſt. In order to which, the widely different Natures and Intereſts of Soul and Body, and of Time and Eternity, ſhould be explained to them, with the Evidences of a future State; and conſequently, of how much Importance it is to them to be, in a good Meaſure, diſengaged from the Body and Time, ſo ſhort and uncertain; and to cultivate the Soul, and improve it in Knowledge and Virtue, of which they can never be diſpoſſeſſed, not even by Death itſelf, they being Treaſures which they can carry with them into another State, and that will laſt for ever. And as our real Well-being depends on *Order*, and as this depends on Law and Rule, of the Fitneſs of which, they are not yet competent Judges; tho' they are to be led to reaſon and judge for themſelves, as faſt as their Capacity will admit of it; in the mean time, they ſhould be taught and inured to Humility, and Obedience to Government, and even to an implicit Obedience, till they are able to judge for themſelves, and be kept, as much as poſſible, from all bad Company, which will be extremely apt to miſlead them.

Of Reading and Writing.

§ 9. AND as it is to be ſuppoſed, that Children have all along, from their firſt Capacity for it, been taught to *read* and *write*, it concerns thoſe who have the Conduct of them, to put them

 upon

upon the Practice of Reading and Writing, particularly with a View at enlarging and improving their Minds, by directing them to read the most instructive and engaging Things in History, Poetry, and Morality, and especially the most instructive and useful Things in the Holy Scriptures; at the same time awakening their Attention to them, and a right Understanding of them: To which Purpose, putting them upon writing out the most striking Passages would be very conducive; as by this Means their Attention would be the more engaged, and they would have a little Treasure of their own of the wisest and most useful Things, and would put the greater Value upon them, under the Notion of their being a Treasure of their own. And, by the Way, Care should be taken, as far as can consist with good Government, to contrive to put and keep them always in a good Humour, which will make every Thing take the better Effect.

Of Musick, Numbers, Figures, Globes, &c.

§ 10. By this Time they may begin to be led to a Sense of the Charms of Musick, and the Mysteries of *Numbers* and geometrical Figures, and the Reasonings and Operations relating to them, as far as their Capacities will admit, which are of the greatest Use, as they tend to ripen their Minds, by inuring them to strong Application, and a close Way of thinking. But Care should be taken that these Exercises do not consist of meer Abstractions, and barren and useless Speculations, but be turned as much as possible to Facts, and Things practical and useful in Life. And by the Time they are ten or twelve Years old, they may be taught from Maps, a general Notion of the Earth,

Earth, the Situation of the ſeveral Countries and Kingdoms upon it, and conſiderable of the Hiſtory of the ſeveral Nations inhabiting it; and at the ſame time, from Schemes and Globes, conſiderable Notion of the Heavens, and the Syſtem of the World in general, as well as this Globe of the Earth in particular: All which, would vaſtly tend to enlarge their Minds, and give them a great and generous Way of Thinking.

Of Grammar, Languages, Oratory, Hiſtory, Poetry, &c.

§ 11. And now if they are deſigned for a publick Education, they are to be taught the Principles of *Grammar* and Language, in which they ſhould, indeed, begin to be initiated by ſix or ſeven Years old; and the Connection between their own and other Languages, ſhould be carefully explained, by inſtructing them in an *Engliſh*, *Latin* and *French* Grammar, at the ſame time: So that by Twelve or Fourteen, they may become pretty well verſed in the Conſtruction of Speech, both *Latin* and *French*, as well as *Engliſh*; and in Two or Three more, of *Greek* and *Hebrew*, that they may be able to read the holy Scriptures in thoſe venerable and noble Languages of Antiquity, in which they were at firſt written, and other excellent Pieces of *Oratory*, *Hiſtory*, *Poetry*, and *Morality*, which were the greateſt Works of Genius, and have ſtood the Teſt of Time, and been handed down to us thro' the ſeveral Ages of Mankind: All which are of great Uſe to refine and poliſh the Mind, and give it a noble Taſte for the ſublimeſt Beauties, as well as the juſteſt Sentiments, and the fineſt Maxims of true Wiſdom; which, therefore ſhould be carefully pointed out, and illuſtrated to them, relating both to Things human and divine: Particularly ſome good *Rhetoric* and *Poetry*, with the *Mythology* of the Ancients, ſhould now be explained, and they ſhould begin to be well verſed in the *Hiſtory* of the World, both *ſacred* and *prophane*, and with it, the Knowledge both of the Times and Places of the ſeveral Facts, from *Geography* and *Chronology*, both ancient and modern. I would have them carried as far as may be in theſe Things by the Time they arrive at the Age of Sixteen or Eighteen.

Of Metaphyſicks, Logick and Criticiſm.

§ 12. AND now it will be time for them to have their Minds cloſely turned inward upon themſelves, to take an exact View of their intellectual Powers, and the Objects of them, by the Studies of *Metaphyſicks* and *Logicks*, in which they are taught the great Principles of firſt Self-evident Truth, and how to make Deductions from them; a thorough Knowledge of the Operations and Procedure of the Mind, and a juſt Notion of right Reaſoning, and of ranging and methodizing their Thoughts, from the ſeveral Relations and Connections of Things. And upon this ſhould at the ſame time be built a more *critical* Knowledge of Language, and its Procedure from literal, to juſt figurative Expreſſions of the Senſe of the Mind; and from the true Art of Reaſoning, which addreſſeth the Underſtanding, to the right Art of Perſuading, in Addreſs to the Paſſions; which ſhould be taught in ſuch a Manner, as to be ſo far from clouding, dazzling and miſguiding the Underſtanding, as to be rather ſubſervient to it, by giving it a clearer Apprehenſion of its Objects, and more ſtrongly engaging its Attention to the

Truth,

Truth, and Right of the Caſe, as well as a Love to it, and Delight in it. To which Purpoſe, the various Stiles in juſt Writing, correſponding to the various Subjects and Purpoſes, ſhould be critically underſtood, and every Thing in Thinking and Speaking be reduced to the Standard of Truth and Nature, without any Sophiſtry, Diſguiſe or falſe Colouring.

Of Mathematicks, & the fine Arts.

§ 13. AND then, from the Doctrine of juſt Reaſoning and exact Speaking, it will be proper, in the next Place, to lead the Mind on to the ſublime *Mathematicks* (the firſt and eaſieſt Things of this Kind, being ſuppoſed to be already known.) And here there opens a ſpacious Field of Certainty and Demonſtration, highly raiſing and improving the Mind in a vaſt Scene of eternal Truths, in the Doctrine of *Numbers* and *Magnitudes*, and their various Proportions; and that wonderful Engine of Mathematical Reaſoning *Algebra*, by the Help of which, the Mind works itſelf into the Diſcovery and Underſtanding of the ſublimeſt Truths, and traverſeth the whole viſible Creation of God, in which all Things are found to be done conformable to thoſe ſublime Principles. And as the Mind is ſuppoſed to have been already converſant in *Eloquence*, *Poetry* and *Muſick*, ſo it ſhould now be led into a Taſte of the other fine Arts, *Painting*, *Sculpture* and *Architecture*, which do in ſome Meaſure depend on the Knowledge of mathematical Proportions.

Of Phyſicks and Aſtronomy.

§ 14. I COULD wiſh the Minds of Children, as I obſerved above, were early initiated in the *Study of Nature*, by being led into the eaſieſt and moſt delightful Things in *Natural Hiſtory*, and a

general

general Survey of the mighty Works of God, both in Heaven and Earth; to which, as they further ripen, their Attention ſhould be now more ſtrongly turned by a Variety of Experiments. And when they are furniſhed with a conſiderable Apparatus in the Skill of mathematical Reaſoning, they ſhould next be taught to apply it in *Phyſicks*, or the Study of Nature, the *Laws of Motion*, Gravitation, Elaſticity, Light, Colours, Sounds and other ſenſible Qualities; and from thence proceed to the Knowledge of every Thing that can be diſcovered in the *Elements*, *Earth*, *Water*, *Air* and *Fire*, and in all the various Tribes of Creatures in this terraqueous Globe, both *Mineral*, *Vegetable* and *Animal*; in all which they muſt be led to take Notice of the wonderful Art, Connections, Deſign and Contrivances that manifeſtly appear in them all, and of every Thing that is uſeful for the Comfort and Elegance of Life, while we continue in this preſent State. And in conſequence of theſe Things, they ſhould be further led on to obſerve and underſtand the *Connection* of this *Globe* itſelf, and all the Creatures in it, with the *Sun*, the Fountain of all Light and Life to the whole Syſtem of the *Planets* and *Comets* belonging to him, and depending on him, and the prodigious Hoſt of *Stars* analogous to him, on whom the like Syſtems may be ſuppoſed to depend, which are the Subjects of *Aſtronomy*. And here, the Contemplation of that World of Things extremely little beneath us, as well as Things vaſtly great, diſtant and remote from us, alike beyond the Ken of the naked Eye, and diſcovered only by the Help of Optic Glaſſes, equally demand their Attention, prodigiouſly enlarge their Imaginations

and

and Underſtandings, and, at the ſame time, lead them to the moſt grand and auguſt Apprehenſions of the DEITY, and of his moſt extenſive Benevolence to all *his whole Family, in Heaven and Earth.* And from a Senſe of the Beauty, Harmony, Order and Uſefulneſs appearing in the whole *Syſtem of Nature*, they are led to a Senſe of the like Beauty, Harmony and Order, which ought to obtain in the *moral Syſtem*, and the Happineſs reſulting from it, which now ſhould be the Subject of their moſt intenſe Study, according to that excellent Saying of *Tully*; *Homo ortus eſt ad mundum contemplandum & imitandum.*

Of Theology and Morals.

§ 15. For as the Mind, from the firſt Dawning of Intellect and Reaſon, hath been ſuppoſed, from the Contemplation of itſelf, and the ſenſible World ſurrounding it, and the Inſtruction of thoſe about it, to be convinced of the Exiſtence of the DEITY, the Author of all Things, and gradually attaining juſt Notions of Him who is the great *Father of Spirits*; ſo now it muſt be led on further, in *Moral Philoſophy*, *Theology*, *Ethics*, &c. to the Contemplation of Him, and that World of Spirits derived from Him, dependent on Him, and ſubjected to his ſupreme Dominion and Government, in which he ſeeks to lead them gradually on thro' a Courſe of Diſcipline, to their higheſt Perfection and Happineſs in their Knowledge of Him, Conformity to Him, and Enjoyment of Him, their ſovereign Good, as the great End of their Exiſtence, and all his Diſpenſations towards them. Here then opens another vaſt Scene of neceſſary and eternal Truths. In order to which, the firſt Study is to gain a right Knowledge of ourſelves, our own intellectual and ac-

tive

tive Powers, our various Affections and Exertions, by Conciousness and Reflection; and thence to form a Notion, not only of other created Spirits, but especially of GOD the great Parent Spirit, by substituting the greatest both natural and moral Perfections we find in ourselves wherewith to conceive of Him and his Dispensations towards us, removing from them all Limitation and Imperfection. And by the intellectual Light wherewith he perpetually irradiateth our Minds, we not only see his absolute Independance and necessary Existence, but also our own intire Dependance on Him, and our Relation and Obligations to Him; from whence evidently resulteth the Fitness, Decency and Duty of all those Affections, and that Behaviour which we manifestly owe to *Him*, and are comprehended under the general Names of *Piety* and *Adoration*. And by the same Light attending our looking inward on ourselves, and considering our own Nature, and our Relations and Connections one with another, we, in like Manner, evidently discern what Affections and Behaviour are fit, decent and due from us to *ourselves*, and to *each other*, implied in the Terms *Moderation*, *Probity* and *Benevolence*; and also that Happiness and Self-enjoyment which resulteth from being conscious of our affecting and behaving accordingly, as well as the Remorse and Misery arising from our affecting and acting otherwise. Thus our Perception of eternal Truth, and Love of Order, in Conformity to it, leadeth the Mind to its Union with the eternal God, and the Happiness of his everlasting Kingdom, in the Conduct and Government of the World, which consisteth in the universal Order, Harmony and Happi-

Happineſs of all intelligent active Beings that are qualified for it.

§ 16. BUT as we are by the Condition of our Natures or Circumſtances, eſpecially the human Species, cantoned out into various particular Societies, it is neceſſary, in order to our Perfection, that we be trained up to act a good Part, under the Diſcipline of theſe Societies in our Progreſs towards it. The firſt is that of the *Family* to which we belong. This leads us to the Study of *OEconomy*, which provideth for the Weal of theſe firſt Rudiments of Society founded in Nature, in which we are to be carried thro' the firſt Stage of Life, and fitted to act a good Part in making a further Progreſs towards our Perfection, under the Diſcipline of the *civil Community* to which we belong, which is founded in Compact, either explicit or tacit, being a voluntary Combination of a great Number of Individuals to promote their Welfare in the common Good of the whole Community; in which, each one is to ſeek his own Weal and Happineſs, both temporal and ſpiritual. Hence ariſeth *Polity*, or the Art of good Government, both *Civil* and *Eccleſiaſtical*; which conſiſteth in the Communities agreeing on certain Rules and Laws founded in the common Intereſt, and enforced by proper Sanctions, in Conformity to which, every Individual is to reſign to the publick or prevailing Senſe (at leaſt as far as his Duty to God will permit) as being the ſafeſt and moſt rational Method he can take, in order to ſecure his own beſt Intereſt and Happineſs. To which, therefore, it will much conduce, that every one be trained up in this Spirit of Reſignation to the publick Senſe, as far as poſſible, and in an ardent Love of the publick

Of Oeconomy and Politicks.

lick Good of his Country and publick Order; in an exact Knowledge of it, and the Laws founded in it, joined with a faithful Conformity to them. And lastly, in an earnest Zeal and Activity in whatever may tend to promote the publick Interest; being constantly taught the Glory of publick Virtue and Usefulness, and deserving well of Mankind.

§ 17. *Of the Intent and Usefulness of Revelation, in improving & advancing us to our highest Perfection.*

BUT as we are attended with innumerable Impressions of Sense, and Solicitations of Imagination and Appetite, continually diverting our Attention and Affections from these Reflections, and the inward Light attending them, and strongly tempting us to the Violation of Order and Law, both moral and political: It must be observed, *lastly*, that God hath from the Beginning, in great Compassion to Mankind, instructed us more perfectly in the Knowledge of these most important Things by *Revelation*, wherein He hath used a Variety of Means to engage our Attention to them, and to reclaim us to Order, and restore us to his Favour, upon our Deviation from them, in order to our true Happiness. And to these Purposes, He hath condescended to accommodate himself to the low Capacities of the general Rate of Mankind, by using various Types and Emblems, and a most beautiful and instructive Language taken from what is familiar among us, wherewith to represent and shadow forth his Perfections and Dispensations, which are vastly above our Comprehension; the Nature and Intent of which Language should be critically considered, and well understood; and the beautiful Analogies drawn

drawn from Things ſenſible and imaginable, to Things intelligible, ſpiritual and moral. Particularly, in the Diſpenſation of his Grace, for our Recovery from the Power and Guilt of Sin, to his Image and Favour, by the Mediation of his Son, and the Influence of his Spirit, It is not his Deſign to teach us preciſe Philoſophical Notions and Verities, as Matters of meer Speculation, but rather chiefly by as exact Conceptions as we are at preſent capable of, borrowed from Things common and familiar to us, to promote in us pure and holy Affections, and all Manner of virtuous Diſpoſitions and Practices; to wean and diſengage us from fleeting and ſenſible Things, and low animal Purſuits and Gratificacations, which we are ſhortly to leave; and to awaken and engage our Attention to ſpiritual, eternal and immutable Things, the Objects of Reaſon and Faith; that we may not *look at the Things that are ſeen, which are temporal, but may look through them to the Things that are not ſeen, which are eternal*; and that we may learn to love and delight in Him, who is *all in all*, our chief and ſovereign Good, and to advance ourſelves to as near a Reſemblance to Him as our Natures will admit of; that by our Conformity to Him, and the Imitation of Him, we may, through the great Mediator, his bleſſed Son, and by the Help of his holy Spirit, be entirely ſecure of his Favour, and for ever happy in Him, ourſelves and one another. Here then we arrive at our *perfect Conſummation and Bliſs*; our higheſt Perfection and Happineſs, both intellectual and moral, in the cleareſt Knowledge of Him and ourſelves, that our Minds can admit of, and the intire Union of our Wills, Affections and Behaviour to

his

his Will, and the Purity and Holineſs of his Nature, and the bleſſed Deſigns of his Kingdom. So that it is by this holy Diſcipline of *Chriſtianity* that we are daily to inure ourſelves to a due Diſengagedneſs from this uncertain ſenſible Scene, and to improve ourſelves in the Knowledge and Love of Things unchangeable and eternal, and in the Exercise of Devotion towards GOD, and the Imitation of Him, till we are qualified to quit this our preſent Station, and enter upon that eternal Life of Contemplation and Devotion, and of univerſal Purity, Probity and Benevolence, which is to be our higheſt Perfection and everlaſting Happineſs in the future State of our Exiſtence.

FINIS.

A BEAUTIFUL

SUMMARY DESCRIPTION OF UNIVERSAL NATURE,

By Biſhop BERKELEY, *in reaſoning againſt the Sceptics, near the Beginning of the* Second *of his* Three Dialogues.

LOOK! Are not the Fields covered with a delightful Verdure? Is there not ſomething in the Woods and Groves, in the Rivers and clear Springs, that ſooths, that ſoftens, that tranſports the Soul? At the Proſpect of the wide and deep Ocean, or ſome huge Mountain, whoſe Top is loſt in the Clouds, or of an old gloomy Foreſt, are not our Minds filled with a pleaſing Horror? Even in the Rocks and Deſarts, is there not an agreeable Wildneſs? How ſincere a Pleaſure is it to behold the natural Beauties of the Earth! To preſerve and renew our Reliſh for them, is not the Veil of Night alternately drawn over her Face, and doth ſhe not change her Dreſs with the Seaſons? How aptly are the Elements diſpoſed? What Variety and Uſe in Stones and Metals, and even in the meaneſt Productions of Nature? What Delicacy, what Beauty, what Contrivance in vegetable and animal Bodies? How exquiſitely are all Things ſuited as well to their

particular Ends, as to conſtitute appoſite Parts of the Whole? And while they mutually aid and ſupport, do they not alſo ſet off and illuſtrate each other? Raiſe now your Thoughts from this Ball of Earth, to all thoſe wondrous Luminaries that adorn the high Arch of Heaven. What an inſupportably ſplendid and glorious Body is the Sun, the Center of this our Syſtem, and the inexhauſtible Fountain of that vaſt ætherial Fluid, which is the Light and Life of this whole Creation? The Motion and Situation of the Planets, are they not admirable for Uſe and Order? Were thoſe (miſcalled *Erratic)* Globes e'er known to ſtray in their repeated Journeys through the pathleſs Void? Do they not meaſure Areas round the Sun, ever proportioned to the Times? So fixed, ſo immutable are the Laws by which the unſeen Author of Nature actuates the Univerſe! How vivid and radiant is the Luſtre of the fixed Stars? How magnificent and rich that negligent Profuſion, with which they appear to be ſcattered throughout the whole azure Vault? Yet if you take the Teleſcope, it brings into your Sight a new Hoſt of Stars that eſcape the naked Eye. Here they ſeem contiguous and minute, but to a nearer View, immenſe Orbs of Light, at various Diſtances, far ſunk in the Abyſs of Space! Now you muſt call Imagination to your Aid. The feeble narrow Senſe cannot deſcry innumerable Worlds revolving round the central Fires; and in thoſe Worlds the Energy of an All-perfect Mind diſplay'd in endleſs Forms! But neither Senſe nor Imagination are big enough to comprehend the boundleſs Extent, with all its glittering Furniture! Though the labouring Mind exert and ſtrain each Power to its utmoſt Reach, there ſtill
ſtands

ſtands out ungraſped a Surpluſage immeaſurable! Yet all the vaſt Bodies that compoſe this mighty Frame, how diſtant and remote ſoever, are by ſome ſecret Mechaniſm, ſome divine Art and Force, linked in a mutual Dependance and Intercourſe with each other; even with this Earth, which was almoſt ſlipt from my Thoughts, and loſt in the Croud of Worlds! Is not the whole Syſtem immenſe, beautiful, glorious, beyond Expreſſion, and beyond Thought? What Treatment then do thoſe Philoſophers deſerve, who would deprive theſe noble and delightful Scenes of all Reality? How ſhould thoſe Principles be entertained, that lead us to think all the viſible Beauty of the Creation a falſe imaginary Glare?

A

PHILOSOPHICAL MEDITATION, OR PRAYER, Of the late Archbishop of *CAMBRAY*:

In his Demonstration of the Existence of GOD, *as it is expressed (nearly) by Bishop* BERKELEY, *in the* Guardian, No. 69.

O My GOD, if the greater Number of Mankind do not discover Thee in that glorious Show of Nature which thou hast placed before our Eyes, it is not because thou art far from every one of us, for it is *in Thee that we live, and move, and have our Being:* Thou art present to us more than any Object which we touch with our Hands, but our Senses and the Passions which they produce in us, turn our Attention from Thee. Thy Light *shines in the midst of Darkness, but the Darkness comprehendeth it not.* Thou, O Lord, dost every where display thyself: Thou shinest forth in all thy Works, but art not regarded by heedless and unthinking Man. The whole

whole Creation talks aloud of Thee, and echoes with the Repetition of Thy holy Name: But ſuch is our Inſenſibility, that we are deaf to the great and univerſal Voice of Nature. Thou art every where about us, and within us, but we wander from ourſelves, become Strangers to our own Souls, and do not apprehend Thy Preſence. O Thou, who art the eternal Fountain of Light and Beauty; who art the Ancient of Days, without Beginning, and without End: O Thou, who art the Life of all that truly live, thoſe can never fail to find Thee who ſeek for Thee within themſelves. But alas! the very Gifts which Thou beſtoweſt upon us do ſo employ our Thoughts, that they divert us from perceiving the Hand that conveys them to us. We live in Thee, and by Thee, and yet we live without thinking of Thee: But, O Lord, what is Life in the Ignorance of Thee? A dead inactive Piece of Matter, a Flower that withers, a River that glides away, a Palace that haſtens to its Ruin, a Picture made up of fading Colours, a Maſs of ſhining Ore; theſe, and ſuch Things as theſe, ſtrike our Imaginations, and make us ſenſible of their Exiſtence, we regard them as Objects capable of giving us Pleaſure, not conſidering that *Thou* conveyeſt to us, *through* them, all the Pleaſure which we imagine *they* give us. Such empty Objects of Senſe as are only the Shadows of Being, take up and engage our low and groveling Thoughts, while that Beauty which Thou haſt poured out on Thy Creation is as a Veil that hides Thee from our Eyes. As Thou art a Being too pure and exalted to paſs thro' our Senſes, Thou art not regarded by Men who have debaſed their Nature, and made them-

themſelves like the Beaſts that periſh. So infatuated are they, that notwithſtanding they know what is Truth and Good, Wiſdom and Virtue, Law and Order, which (tho' the moſt real and ſtable Things) have neither Figure, nor Colour, nor Sound, nor Taſte, nor Smell, nor any other ſenſible Quality, yet they can doubt of Thy Exiſtence, becauſe Thou art not apprehended by the groſſer Organs of Senſe. Wretches that we are! we conſider Shadows as Realities, and Truth as a Phantom: That which is nothing is all to us, and that which is all appears to us as nothing. But what do we ſee in all Nature but Thee, O my God? Thou and only Thou appeareſt in every Thing. When I conſider Thee, O Lord, I am ſwallowed up, and loſt in the Contemplation of Thee. Every Thing beſides Thee, even my own Exiſtence, vaniſhes and diſappears in Contemplation of Thee: I am aſtoniſhed and fall into nothing when I think of Thee! The Man who does not ſee Thee has beheld nothing: He who does not taſte Thee has a Reliſh of nothing; his Being is vain, and his Life but a Dream. How unhappy is that Soul who without the Senſe of Thee has no God, no Hope, no Comfort to ſupport him? On the contrary, how happy is the Man that ſearches, ſighs and thirſts after Thee? But he only is fully happy, on whom thou lifteſt up the Light of Thy Countenance, and who, being conformed to Thee, enjoys in Thy loving Kindneſs the Completion of all his Deſires. Thou therefore, O my God, art the God of my Life, my Joy and my Hope: *Thou wilt guide me with Thy Counſel, and afterward receive me to Glory: Thou wilt ſhew me the Path of of Life ; in thy Presence is Fulness of Joy, and at thy right Hand there are Pleasures for evermore. Whom then have I in Heaven but Thee ? And there is nothing in Earth that I will desire in Comparison of thee. My Flesh and my Heart faileth : But Thou, O my G O D, art the Strength of my Heart, and my Portion for ever.*

The E N D.

A more accurate TABLE, for the Partition of the Sciences, than that, Page xix.

CYCLOPÆDIA, is the whole Circle of Learning, or the Knowledge of every Thing that may contribute to our Happiness, both in Theory and Practice, and consists of two Parts.

- I. *Philology*, or the Study of Language or *Signs*, called also *Humanity*, and the *Belles Lettres*, and is,
  - 1. *General*, or common to all Kinds of Speaking, in
    - 1. *Grammar*, of pure Language.
    - 2. *Rhetorick*, of figurative Speech.
  - 2. *Special*, of particular Kinds of Speaking or Writing, as
    - 1. *Oratory*, which treats of Eloquence.
    - 2. *History*, which relates real Facts.
    - 3. *Poetry*, which describes Things in an elevated Manner, whether real or imaginary; and to all these belongs the Art of *Criticism*.
- II. *Philosophy*, or the Study of Wisdom, being the Knowledge of *Things*, together with Practice correspondent thereto, in both which consists our Happiness. All Things or Beings are,
  - 1. *Bodies*, or sensible Things, which constitute the natural World, the Knowledge of which is, in a large Sense, called *Physicks*, or *Natural Philosophy*, and is,
    - 1. *General*, of the common Affections of Bodies, Number and Magnitude, in *Mathematicks*, including *Arithmetick* and *Geometry*.
    - 2. *Special*, of all particular Things in the natural World: Particularly,
      - 1. *Natural History*, which gives an Account of Facts in all Nature.
      - 2. *Mechanicks*, of the Laws of Motion.
      - 3. *Geology*, of this terraqueous Globe, and all Things in it, inanimate and animate. And,
      - 4. *Astronomy*, of the Heavens and Stars, and the whole Mundane System.
    - Under each of which Heads there are many practical Matters.
  - Or, 2. *Spirits*, or intelligent moral Beings, which constitute the intelligent or moral World, the Knowledge of which, in a large Sense of the Words, may be called *Metaphysics*, and *Moral Philosophy*, and is,
    - First, *Speculative*, or what relates to the Knowledge of intellectual Things.
      - 1. In *General*, the *Noetics* or *Logic*, including both *Ontology* and *Dialectic* of the Conduct of the Mind in Thinking or Reasoning.
      - 2. In *Special*, *Pneumatology*, of the several Kinds of created Intelligences.
      - 3. *Theology*, of the DEITY, the Father and Lord of them all.
    - Second, *Practical*, or what relates to Life and Conduct, in our several Capacities, personal and social.
      - 1. *Ethics*, of the Conduct of our Temper and Behaviour in general, in order to Happiness.
      - 2. *OEconomics*, of the Conduct of Families. And,
      - 3. *Politics*, of the Government of States, *Civil* and *Ecclesiastical*; to which relate *Biography*, and *Civil* and *Ecclesiastical History*.

A SHORT SYSTEM OF MORALS.

ETHICA:

Or the First PRINCIPLES of

Moral Philosophy;

And especially that Part which is called

ETHICS.

In a CHAIN of necessary CONSEQUENCES from certain FACTS.

Remember this, and shew yourselves Men. ISAIAH xlvi. 8.

This is your reasonable Service. St. PAUL, ROM. xii. 1.

Hæc tractanti animo, & noctes & dies cogitanti, existit illa a Deo Delphis *præcepta cognitio, ut* Ipsa se mens agnoscat, *conjunctamque cum Mente Divinâ se sentiat; ex quo, insatiabili Gaudio completur.* CIC. TUSC. DISP.

Discite, O miseri! Et causas cognoscite rerum,
Quid sumus? Et quidnam victuri gignimur? Ordo
Quis datus?——Quem Te Deus esse
Jussit? Et humanâ quâ parte locatus es in Re?
PERS. SAT. 3.

The SECOND EDITION.

PHILADELPHIA:
Printed by B. FRANKLIN, and D. HALL, at the *New-Printing-Office*, near the Market. 1752.

ADVERTISEMENT.

W*HAT is here attempted, is a ſhort Syſtem of* Ethics *or* Morals *(chiefly for the Uſe of young Beginners) which have, of late, been called* The Religion of Nature; *by which I would not be underſtood to mean a Syſtem of Truths and Duties which meer* natural Reaſon *would ever, of itſelf, have diſcovered, in the preſent Condition of Mankind, without the Aſſiſtance of* Revelation *or Inſtruction; for it is but a very little of GOD and Religion, or of Truth and Duty, that Man, in his preſent State, utterly uninſtructed, is able to diſcover by his meer natural Powers, as the Fact hath abundantly demonſtrated, where the ancient Inſtructions were loſt. Nor can it, indeed, be imagined, from the Goodneſs of GOD, that when he firſt brought Man into Being, a Stranger to every Thing about him, that he would leave him to grope out every Thing that was neceſſary, or even expedient, in order to anſwer the End of his Being, his true Happineſs, without Inſtruction, even in Language and Nature, as well as Religion and Morals; or, that when he had been ſurprized by a Temptation, and fallen into Sin, that he would leave him to periſh without giving him further Inſtructions, to be handed down to his Poſterity, how he and they ſhould return to their Duty, and regain His Favour. And that the Fact was accordingly, we are aſſured from the moſt ancient Accounts of the firſt Condition of Mankind. What I would therefore be underſtood to mean by* Ethics, *or* the Religion of Nature, *is, That Syſtem of Truths and Duties, which, tho' they are not obvious to our weak Rea-*

ſon

ſon, without Revelation or Inſtruction, yet when diſcovered, whether by the one or the other, do evidently appear, upon due Conſideration, to be founded in the firſt Principles of Reaſon and Nature; in the Nature of GOD and Man, and the various Relations that ſubſiſt between them; and from thence to be capable even of ſtrict Demonſtration.

WE know there are a great Number of Truths in Mathematicks *and* Natural Philoſophy, *which not One in Ten Thouſand of the Bulk of Mankind would ever have thought of, if it had not been for ſuch great Men as* Euclid, Apollonius, Archimedes *and Sir* Iſaac Newton, *&c. which yet may, ſafely, and with great Advantage, be received upon their Authority, and be accordingly practiſed upon, by thoſe who have not Leiſure or Ability to attend to the Reaſons of them: And now they have led the Way, it is not very difficult for thoſe, who are capable of thinking cloſely, to enter into the Demonſtrations of them: The Caſe is much the ſame as to moral Truths and Duties, with regard to the Authority of Prophets and Law-givers. It is the Part of the Prophet or Law-giver, as ſuch, to diſcover Truths, and enjoin Laws, as Rules of Behaviour to the People, who are to receive them upon their Authority, as having but little Leiſure or Capacity to exerciſe their Reaſon about them, and therefore act rationally in ſo doing: And it is the Part of the* Philoſopher, *as ſuch, as far as it is practicable, to enter into the Reaſons and Demonſtrations, on which thoſe Truths and Duties are originally founded.*

SUCH a ſhort Delineation of Morals, *may, perhaps, be of ſome Uſe, eſpecially in theſe Times, wherein there is a Sect ariſen, or rather revived, that is continually decrying* Morality, *as tho' it were only carnal Reaſon, and no Part of* Chriſtiani-

ty,

ty, *nor ſcarce conſiſtent with it: This, it may be preſumed, they would ſcarcely do, if they duly conſidered what* Morality *truly is. And, on the other Hand, as one Extreme is apt to beget another, it is to be feared there may be another Sect ariſing, or gaining Ground, who from too juſt an Indignation at thoſe abſurd Notions of* Chriſtianity, *are in Danger, for want of due Conſideration, of not only ſetting light by* that, *but even of loſing all ſerious Senſe of the true Extent and Obligations of* Morality *itſelf. It is therefore the Deſign of the following Pages, to endeavour to give a juſt Notion of it, and the Reaſons on which it is founded, and to ſhew its Extent and vaſt Importance, and what Connection there is between* it *and* Chriſtianity.

I would only advertiſe this one Thing further; That no Speculation or Demonſtration whatſoever, is of any further real Uſe to us, than ſo far forth as it directs or engages us in Life and Practice, on which our Happineſs all depends. And, as our Reaſon in theſe Things, is, at beſt, but very dark and weak, it is of the greateſt Importance to us, that we diligently ſtudy the holy Oracles, in which we have the ſublimeſt and moſt advantageous Inſtructions and Incentives to Practice, with regard to theſe Matters, which are of the utmoſt Importance to our true and everlaſting Happineſs. However, as we are reaſonable Creatures, and obliged, as ſuch, to yield unto GOD, *the Author of our Beings, a* reaſonable Service, *it may be of very good Uſe for us, as far as it will go, with an implicit Submiſſion to Him for the reſt, to exerciſe our Reaſon upon theſe great and important Subjects.*

THE CONTENTS.

INTRODUCTION.

PART I.

The Speculative Part *of* MORAL PHILOSOPHY.

PART II.

The Practical Part *of* MORAL PHILOSOPHY.

N. B. There are several Principles of Reasoning supposed in the following Tract, as having been known from the *Noetica*: However, as this may fall into some Hands that have not that Tract, I hope I may be excused, if there be in this some Repetitions.

ETHICS:

ETHICS:

OR

Moral Philoſophy.

THE

INTRODUCTION.

Of the Nature of Ethics, *or* Moral Philoſophy, *in general.*

1. AS *Natural Philoſophy* is the Knowledge of the natural World, or the World of Bodies, and the general Laws of the corporeal Nature, together with all thoſe practical Matters thereon depending, that promote our comfortable Subſiſtence and Well-being in this preſent State; ſo *Moral Philoſophy* is the Knowledge of the moral World; the World of Spirits, or intelligent free Agents, and the general Laws of the moral Nature; together with all that practical Conduct and Behaviour thereon depending, that is neceſſary to promote our true Happineſs, both in our preſent and future State. And as the *NOETICA* imply all thoſe Inſtructions and Means, that relate to the Improvement and Conduct of our

Underſtandings in Purſuit of the Knowledge of Truth: So the *ETHICA* imply all thoſe Inſtructions and Means that relate to the Regulation and Conduct of our Affections, Actions and Behaviour, in Purſuit of the Enjoyment of our true and chief Good.

2. THE World of intelligent free Agents, indeed, comprehends the whole Syſtem of created Spirits, both Angels and Men, and whatever other Species there may be, conſidered as being derived from, and under the Conduct and Government of Almighty GOD, the Author, the Father and Lord of all. But what I mean chiefly to inſiſt upon, is, the *Knowledge of ourſelves*, as we are *Men*, or a moral Syſtem of rational Animals, in all the Relations wherein we ſtand, both with regard to GOD, ourſelves, and one another, with a Behaviour ſuitable thereunto (without conſidering us particularly either in our *œconomical* or *political* Capacities) which is the Foundation of all the reſt, and is uſually termed *Ethics*.

3. *ETHICS* is the Art of living happily, by the right Knowledge of ourſelves, and the Practice of Virtue: Our *Happineſs* being the End, and *Knowledge* and *Virtue*, the Means to that End.

4. WE are ſaid to live happily when we enjoy ourſelves, and all that is really good for us, in the whole of our Nature and Duration; *i. e.* conſidered, not only as ſenſitive, but as reaſonable, free, active, ſocial and immortal Creatures. For *Happineſs* means that Pleaſure which ariſeth in us from our Enjoyment of ourſelves, and all that is really good for us, or ſuitable to our Natures, and conducive to our Happineſs in the whole.

5. THE

5. The Enjoyment of ourſelves, and all that is truly good, depends on a good Habit, or State of the Soul, united with, and delighting in its proper Objects, which are *Truth* and *Good*; the firſt being the Object of the Underſtanding, and the other of the Will and Affections: And this good Habit is the ſame Thing with *Virtue*.

6. *VIRTUE* conſiſts in that Integrity, Firmneſs and Stability of the Soul, whereby we do honeſtly and ſtedfaſtly perſiſt, in ſpite of all Temptations to the contrary, in the Love and Practice of *moral Good*, and the Hatred and Forbearance of *moral Evil*: *Vice* is the contrary.

7. *MORAL Good* conſiſts in freely chuſing and doing whatſoever Truth and right Reaſon dictate as neceſſary to be choſen and done, in order to our true Happineſs: *Moral Evil* the contrary; for moral Good muſt mean, the Good of a moral Agent; *i. e.* of[a] rational, conſcious, free, ſelf-exerting and ſelf-determining Agent.

8. There are two Things neceſſary to be conſidered, with reſpect to the Nature of *moral Good*: *viz.* The *Criterion*, or Teſt, by which, in the right Uſe of our Reaſon, we determine what we ought to do, or forbear; and the *Obligations* we thereupon find ourſelves under to the Practice of it.

9. (I.) The *Criterion* or Teſt, whereby we determine what we ought to do or forbear, or what thoſe Actions and Forbearances are, which are to be choſen and done, is the *natural Good* of them, or that Pleaſure and Happineſs in the whole of our Nature and Duration, which naturally attends them: For we find by Experience, that ſome Things, Affections and Actions, are, in the very Nature of them, attended with Pleaſure

or Happineſs, either to the Mind, as perceptive of Truth, or to the Will and Affections, as deſirous of Good; and others with Pain or Miſery, in reſpect to the one or the other. In ſome we have a quick Senſe of the Decent and Amiable, which delight the Mind; and in others, of the Deformed and Odious, which diſpleaſe it: In ſome we perceive the Advantage, in others the Miſchief attending them, to ourſelves or others; and accordingly, the former are attended with inward Tranquility, Acquieſcence, and Self-approbation, and the latter with Anxiety, Remorſe, and Self-reproach. And as Eaſe, Pleaſure or *Happineſs*, is what we call *natural Good*; ſo Uneaſineſs, Pain or *Miſery*, we call *natural Evil.*

10. But in order to make a right Judgment of *natural Good* and *Evil*, as being the Teſt of *moral*, we muſt (as I ſaid) take into the Account, the *whole of our Nature and Duration*, as being *ſenſitive* and *rational*, *ſocial* and *immortal* Creatures. It muſt therefore be the Good and Happineſs of the *whole human Nature*, and the *whole moral Syſtem*, in *Time*, and to all *Eternity*. Hence the Good of the *animal Body*, or the *Pleaſure of Senſe*, is but imaginary, and ceaſeth to be *Good*, and hath even the Nature of *Evil*, ſo far forth as it is inconſiſtent with the Good and Happineſs of the *Soul:* Which is alſo the Caſe of *private Good*, ſo far forth as it is inconſiſtent with the *Good* of the *Publick*; and *temporal Good*, ſo far forth as it is inconſiſtent with that which is *eternal.*

11. And this our *Good* and Happineſs in the whole, does neceſſarily coincide with, and even reſult from, the *Truth* and *Nature* of Things, or Things, Affections and Actions, conſidered as being

being what they really are;* for thus to consider them, is the same Thing with considering them as being *fit*, and tending, in the *Nature* of them, to render our rational, social and immortal *Nature*, in the whole ultimately happy: And such Affections and Actions, correspondent to such Natures and Characters, must be necessarily and eternally fit; it being impossible to conceive of such Natures and Relations, but such moral Affections and Actions will result as *fit* and *right*, and the contrary, as *unfit* and *wrong*. So that the *general Good* of the whole, the *Nature* and *Fitness* of Things, and *the Truth* of Things, or Things considered as being what they are, are, as I apprehend, really coincident, and do, in Effect, come to the same Thing, in settling the Criterion of *Right* and *Wrong*, or the Test whereby we must determine what we are to chuse or avoid, and to do or forbear.

12. *MORAL Good* must therefore consist in freely chusing and acting conformable to the *Truth* and *Nature* of *Things*; or to Things, Affections and Actions, considered as being what *they* really are, *i. e.* as tending, or not tending to our true Happiness, as being what *we* really are: Or (which is the same Thing) in chusing and acting according to the *Fitness of Things*, or to Things, Affections and Actions, considered as fit or subservient, in their own Nature, to promote our best *Good* and Happiness *in the whole*. And this again is the same Thing with acting according to *right Reason* (which has been sometimes called the *Criterion*) it being by the right Use of our Reason that we apprehend Things

* Vide *Clarke*, and *Wollaston*.

as being what they really are, and discover which those Things, Affections and Actions are, that do, in the Nature of them, tend to our true Happiness in the whole; and thereby judge what we must do and avoid, and form Rules by which we must act in all our Conduct and Behaviour, so as to be truly happy.

13. (II.) THE *Obligation* we are under, as moral Agents, to practise accordingly, implieth some *Law*, binding us, under certain Penalties, to such Actions as are morally Good, and to forbear the contrary; and this constitutes the Notions of *Duty* and *Sin*, and is two-fold, *Natural* and *Internal*, or *External* and *Moral*.

14. (I.) THE *natural* and *internal* Obligation to the Practice of moral Virtue ariseth from the *Law* of our *Nature*, or that Law which GOD hath established within our own Breasts, and in the Frame of our Nature. And this is the Law of *Reason* and *Conscience*, together with the Law of *Self-love*, and *Self-preservation*, and the Law of *Benevolence*.

15. (1.) THE Law of *Reason* and *Conscience* is, I think, the same Thing which some have called the *moral Sense*, * being a kind of quick and almost intuitive Sense of Right and Wrong, deriving, as I conceive, from the perpetual Presence and Irradiation of the Deity in our Minds, and dictating with a strong and commanding Force what is reasonable, fair and decent, and so fit and right to be done, and giving us Applause and Satisfaction when we conform to it, and blaming and reproaching us, and filling us with Uneasiness and Remorse, when we act contrary to

* Vide *Shaftsbury*, *Hutcheson*, and *Preceptor*, or *Turnbull*.

to its Dictates: It being the Law of our Nature, that we ſhould always affect and act conformable to the inward Senſe of our own Minds and Conſciences. And thoſe conſequent pleaſing or uneaſy Sentiments, conſidering it as a Law, are its Sanctions.

16. (2.) The Law of *Self-love* and *Self-preſervation*, which makes us ſolicitous for the Continuance of our Exiſtence, and the Enjoyment of ourſelves, and ariſeth from the Conſciouſneſs of our Exiſtence, and of Pleaſure or Pain, naturally attending certain Conditions in which we are, or may be, or the contrary; which therefore are its Sanctions. For it is manifeſt that we are, by the Author of our Nature, laid under a Neceſſity of valuing ourſelves and our own *Intereſt*, and of ſeeking and purſuing our own *Preſervation* and *Well-being* or Happineſs, and whatever we find tends to it, or is connected with it; and conſequently that of the Society to which we belong, with which we find our own is, in the Nature of Things, neceſſarily connected.

17. From whence ariſeth (thirdly) the Law of *Benevolence*, or that Diſpoſition we find alſo implanted in us towards the Good of others, ariſing from Reflection, whereby we are led to put ourſelves in each other's Stead, and to have a ſecret Pleaſure or Uneaſineſs in the good or ill Condition of others, from a Conſciouſneſs of our own, in the like Situation; which Sentiments therefore are its Sanctions. This Principle makes us deſirous of each other's Eſteem and Goodwill, and puts us upon doing what we know may be pleaſing and advantageous to each other, and to the whole; ſo that *ſelf* and *ſocial Good* can-

not be considered in themselves, as at all interfering, but as being intirely coincident and subservient to each other.

18. BUT while we rest here, and act upon no other Views or Motives than these *Laws of our Nature* suggest, without considering them as being the Laws of the GOD (or the Author) of Nature; though what we do, may be said, according to the common Acceptation, to be meerly *morally good* or *evil*, and *virtuous* or *vicious*; yet there will be nothing in it (however firm and stable our Conduct be) that can properly be called *Religion*, which must ever enter into the just and complete Notion of *Morality*; for this must be understood to comprehend every Thing that can either direct or influence our moral Behaviour, and consequently must consider us in all the Relations wherein we stand, not only to ourselves and one another, but, above all, to the great Author of our Being, on whom we do intirely depend, and to whom we are therefore, in all Reason, accountable.

19. (II.) The *external* and *moral Obligation* we are under to those Actions and Forbearances above-mentioned, ariseth from *moral Government*, or the Consideration that they are the Will and Law of a Superior who aims at our Happiness in enjoying them, to whom we are therefore accountable for our Behaviour, and by whom we shall be rewarded or punished; *i. e.* made to feel Pleasure or Pain, according as we behave well or ill (which are its Sanctions:) So that this Obligation takes its Force from the former, and this is two-fold, *political* and *religious*.

20. (1.) THE *political Obligation* to the Practice

tice of theſe moral Actions and Forbearances, is the Conſideration that they are the publick Will, or the Will and *Law of the Society* or Government we live under, and to which we are accountable (whether indeed it be a *Family* or a *State*) enforced by the Sanctions of temporal Rewards and Puniſhments. In this View *moral Laws* become *political Laws*, and *moral Good*, *political Good*, to which many other might be added, for promoting of the publick Weal.

21. But here again, tho' GOD is the Founder of Government, both œconomical and political, yet while we reſt on this Foot, and act meerly under theſe political Views, and with a Regard only to our Intereſt in this World, tho' we may be ſaid to be meer *moral Men* (as that Expreſſion is commonly uſed) or *good Citizens*, and *good Common-wealthſmen*, we cannot be ſaid to be *religious*, no, not even in thoſe Actions that relate to GOD himſelf. But,

22. (2.) The *religious Obligation* we are under to thoſe Actions and Forbearances that are neceſſary to our Happineſs in the whole, is the Conſideration that they are the Will and *Law of GOD*, our Creator, Preſerver, and ſupreme moral Governor, the great Author, Head and Lord of the whole ſocial Syſtem, enforced by the Sanctions of *eternal Rewards* and *Puniſhments*, to whom we are juſtly accountable for all our Behaviour, and by whom we muſt expect to be treated well or ill, according as that ſhall be found to be good or bad.

23. For it will appear hereafter, that they muſt be the Will and Law of GOD concerning us, becauſe He being perfectly happy, and Self-ſuffi-

sufficient to his own Happiness, cannot aim at any Advantage to himself, in giving us Being, or in any of his Dispensations towards us; and consequently, that his great End must be our Happiness; and that this he will consider as *his* Interest, his Delight and Glory, that his rational Creatures be in the whole, a happy System, by doing what is fit and right upon all Occasions. It being therefore his Aim that we be happy, whatsoever does, in the Nature of it, and according to the Constitution which he hath made, tend to his Honour and our true Happiness, as being therefore fit and right, must be his *Will* and *Law* concerning us, and consequently our *Duty*, and what is contrary thereto, must be *Sin*.

24. THAT, therefore, which constitutes the Nature of *Religion*, and denominates our Actions and Behaviour *religious*, and makes *Religion* and *Morality*, in the complete Notion of it, coincident, is, That we forbear whatsoever tends to our Misery, and do every Thing that tends to our Happiness in the whole, in Obedience to the Will of GOD, and from a Sense of Duty to Him, and in View of his All-seeing Eye, and the Account we are to give of ourselves to Him.

25. So that upon the whole it appears, That *Morality*, in the just Extent of it, is the same Thing with the *Religion of Nature*, or that *Religion* which is founded in the *Nature* of Things; and that it may be defined, *the Pursuit of our true Happiness by Thinking, Affecting and Acting, according to the Laws of Truth and right Reason, under a Sense of the Duty that we owe to Almighty GOD, and the Account we must expect to give of ourselves to Him.* * Since therefore *Truth* and *Duty*

* Vide *Crousaz's Art of Thinking*, Page 60. Vol. 1.

Duty are thus neceſſarily connected, it muſt be our Buſineſs in this Eſſay, to ſearch out all the *Truths* that relate both to *ourſelves*, to *GOD*, and our *Fellow Creatures*, and thence to deduce the ſeveral *Duties* that do neceſſarily reſult from them.

26. Now theſe may be all reduced to that grand ancient Principle of true Wiſdom, *Know thyſelf*; which muſt imply, not meerly the Knowledge of ourſelves, ſingly conſidered, but alſo in all the Relations wherein we ſtand; for this is the Knowledge of ourſelves in the whole: And becauſe we are *active* as well as *intelligent* Creatures, and our Happineſs depends on *Action* as well as *Thinking*, it muſt therefore be underſtood to mean a *practical Knowledge*. I ſhall accordingly explain this Enquiry under theſe *ſix* following Heads, which, in order the better to bring them down into Life and Action, I chuſe to expreſs them generally in the firſt Perſon, or in the Manner of a Converſation with ourſelves; which Method may, perhaps, be moſt uſeful, in order to teach young People how to reaſon with themſelves upon theſe great and important Subjects to the beſt Advantage.

27. LET therefore every one, in order to the right Knowledge of *himſelf*, and his *Duty* and *Happineſs*, and that he may the more effectually be engaged in Practice, thus ſeriouſly reflect and enquire concerning himſelf. I. *What am I?* II. *How came I to be what I am?* III. *For what End was I made and have my Being?* IV. *What ought I immediately to do, and be, in order to anſwer the End of my Being?* V. *Whether I am what I ought to be?*----If not, VI. *What ought I to*

I to do, as a Means, in order to be and do what I ought, and in order finally to anſwer the End of my Being? The *three firſt* of theſe Enquiries will diſcover the *Truths*; and the *three laſt*, the *Duties*, that we are concerned to know and do in order to our true Happineſs: And the *Truths* are the *ſpeculative*, and the *Duties* are the *practical* Part of *Moral Philoſophy*.

PART

PART I.

The *Speculative* PART of MORAL PHILOSOPHY.

CHAP I.

Of the Nature of Man, *his* Excellencies *and* Imperfections.

§ 1. (I.) IT is *first* necessary that we consider the *Truths* contained in the *Speculative* Part of this Science, relating to *GOD* and *ourselves*: And as we take our Rise to the Knowledge of GOD and his Conduct towards us, from the Knowledge of ourselves, and our Intercourse one with another; we must therefore begin with this, and in order hereunto, let every one seriously ask himself this Question; I. *What am I?* A Question that I doubt few seriously think of, or much concern themselves about, and so live and die great Strangers to themselves, however near and dear that *Self* of ours is to us! And that he may duly answer this Enquiry, let him thus consider and reason with himself.

§ 2. As I am certain from the Perceptions and Operations of my own Mind, that *I am*, or have a Being; so I know that I am not a *Stock*, a *Stone*,

Stone, or a *Tree*; for they have manifestly no Sense or Activity: Whereas I am conscious that I can *see*, *hear*, *taste*, *smell* and *feel*, and enjoy *Pleasure*, and suffer *Pain*, and can spontaneously *exert* myself, and *act* and move from Place to Place, in Pursuance of the one, which I *love* and *delight* in, and for avoiding of the other, which I *hate* and *dread*. All which are much nobler Powers and Faculties than those inanimate Beings are furnished with.

§ 3. NOR yet am I a *Beast*, a *Horse*, a *Dog*, or an *Ox*, &c. for tho' they appear to see, hear, *&c.* and to feel Pleasure and Pain as I do, and can move themselves spontaneously from Place to Place; yet they have but low, groveling Sensations, Exertions and Enjoyments. They appear to have no Notion of any Thing but the Objects of Sense, can conceive nothing of Duty and Sin, and seem capable of no Enjoyment of any Thing but Meat and Drink, and the Means of continuing their Species, and defending themselves; and these only are the Things to which their Exertions and Activity tend.

§ 4. WITH Regard to these, they have, indeed, a wonderful Sagacity, and what looks like Reasoning, Design and Contrivance, and a social Tendency; but these do not seem to be any Thing of their own, because they have them originally, and do not acquire them by Teaching, Trial and Industry. This Sagacity therefore seems to be what we call an *Instinct*; by which Word, nothing else can be meant, but that they are rather passively acted and conducted by some other Being; some governing Mind on whom they depend, according to certain Laws of Nature which He hath established, than that they act from

from any Principle of Deliberation and Design within themselves.

§ 5. THESE Sensations, Appetites and Exertions, indeed, I find I have in common with them; but then I am conscious of vastly nobler Powers and Faculties than these. For I find I can *reflect* and look into my own Mind, and consider myself and my own Powers and Actions, and their Objects: I can attend to the Light of the *pure Intellect*, and *compare* one Thing with another, and observe their several *Relations*, and abstract and give general Names. I can *judge* of True and False, and of Right and Wrong, and deliberate and weigh Things, and *reason* and infer one Thing from another, and reduce them into *Method* and Order, according to their various Connections and Dependences. I can *excite* Imaginations and Conceptions of Things past or absent, and recollect them in my Mind at Pleasure, and reject or *keep* them under my Consideration as I please, at least in a good Measure, and am at *Liberty* to suspend judging till I have carefully examined them, and to *act*, or not to act, in Consequence of my Deliberations, as I think fit. In the Impressions of Sense indeed, and the Perceptions of Evidence, I am passive, but in all these I am evidently active, and can chuse or refuse, will or nill, act or forbear, from a Principle of Self-exertion; which are all truly great and noble Powers.

§ 6. I CAN, moreover, in Consequence of these Abilities, contrive and project *Ends* and *Means*, and Reasons of acting, and *Rules* to act by, and foresee much of the Events of my Conduct. I can give *Laws*, and propose Motives to myself or others, and exact an Account of

myself

myſelf or them, and give an Account to myſelf or others, whether I or they do, or do not act according to thoſe Laws. And I find, that as I *love* or *hate* Things according as they are agreeable or diſagreeable to me; ſo I have *Hopes* or *Fears*, *Joys* or *Griefs*, according as I feel, or have in View, Pleaſures or Pains, and am *conſcious* of having done well or ill, and that my own *Conſcience* will not fail to *juſtify* and *applaud*, or *accuſe* and *condemn* me accordingly; and as I feel great *Joy* and *Satisfaction* in having done what I apprehend to be right, ſo I feel no leſs *Shame*, *Horror*, and *Remorſe*, when I have done what is wrong.

§ 7. From hence I not only know that I have a Being, but alſo that when I am in tolerable Circumſtances, and do well, I have a great Enjoyment of that Being; that it is very dear to me, and that I am, above all Things, concerned to preſerve and continue it, and to make it as comfortable and happy as ever I can; and am therefore deſirous to acquire and enjoy all the Means and Accommodations, the Goods of the Mind, Body or Fortune, that are neceſſary and convenient for that Purpoſe; which I have alſo a great Value for, in Proportion to their Subſerviency to that End, and am very *fearful* of being deprived, and very apt to be *diſpleaſed* or feel Reſentment at any One that would deprive me of them, and *grateful* to any One that does any Thing towards furniſhing me with them, or ſecuring them to me. And all theſe Deſires and Affections of the *private Kind*, are evidently planted in our Nature to be ſubſervient to our perſonal Subſiſtence and Well-being.

§ 8. And

§ 8. AND as I can look back and remember what I have been knowing to in my Time; so I can imagine a Time when I was not, and conceive a Notion of a great Number of Ages and Transactions before me, and of an endless Succession of Ages and Transactions to come. And I can, ot only conceive that I may, but cannot refrain from being earnestly desirous, in some Condition or other, to bear a Part in them, and to enjoy myself happily through all imaginable Periods of Duration: So that though I know there must have been a Time when I began to be, yet I am solicitous that I may never cease to be, and to enjoy myself; and cannot avoid having Hopes of this, even after Death, since this Life turns to but little Account. All these are so many Facts, and I am conscious and intuitively certain of them, if I look carefully within myself. And such are the Properties of my *Soul* or *Spirit*, which is properly *myself*, my reasonable and active Nature.

§ 9. BUT besides these Things which relate to my *Soul (myself*, or *spiritual Nature)* I find that I have a wonderfully contrived, and admirably useful Engine, *my Body*, which I constantly carry about me, and animate throughout (being tied and confined to it by the present Laws of my Nature) consisting of a vast Number and Variety of Parts and Organs, exquisitely framed and fitted to each other, and to all the Functions, Powers and Operations of my Soul; my Eyes to see, my Ears to hear, my Tongue to speak, my Hands to handle, and my Feet to walk, *&c.* (not to mention a thousand Instances of the most wise Design and Contrivance, in all the inward Parts throughout, for all the Purposes of the

Animal Œconomy, which are not immediately ſubject to my own Will and Activity.) Upon the Account of which, as well as the abovementioned Powers of my Soul, I muſt confeſs that, however I came to be, I am indeed *fearfully and wonderfully made.*

§ 10. I alſo find, upon looking about me, an endleſs Variety of ſenſible Objects; a glorious Heaven above me, and a ſpacious Earth beneath me, furniſhed with a ſurprizing Variety of Inhabitants, all connected (together with my own Body, one of the moſt curious Machines of them all) in a moſt wonderful Manner one with another. So that it is manifeſt from their Dependence and Subſerviency, that they are contrived and deſigned to conſtitute, as in Fact they do, one harmonious, beautiful and uſeful Syſtem; one complete and intire Whole; in which I find every Thing fitted, in the beſt Manner, to my own Conveniencies and Pleaſures, both for the comfortable Subſiſtence of my Body, and the Entertainment and Delight of my Soul; but ſo, that it was, at the ſame time, the manifeſt Deſign of them to excite, engage, direct and employ my Activity, without which I find I cannot comfortably enjoy either myſelf or them.

§ 11. I CAN moreover carry my Thoughts and Imaginations throughout the vaſt Spaces of Heaven and Earth, and have a mighty Curioſity to pry and ſearch out the Secrets and Laws of Nature, and diſcover and conceive, as much as I can, of the great Author of it, and what Sort of Behaviour and Conduct is ſuitable to my Nature, and the Relation I ſtand in to Him and my Fellow Creatures, as tending to make me and them happy, and as ſuch, muſt be amiable, and cannot

cannot fail of approving itſelf, not only to my own Reaſon and Conſcience, but alſo to Him and all reaſonable Beings, whoſe Eſteem and good Will I am, from a Tendency founded in Nature itſelf, very ſolicitous to obtain. (*Introd.* 15. 16. 17.)

§ 12. Of which, as I know there are a great Number of my own Kind, ſo I cannot reaſonably doubt but there are others of various Orders above me, which may probably have other and nobler Senſes than thoſe five narrow Inlets that I am acquainted with, and confined to, and far greater and nobler Abilities, both of Underſtanding and Activity, than I am furniſhed with. Such I can eaſily conceive to be poſſible; and, from the various Gradations in Perfection of Being, in the ſeveral Tribes below me, it is very probable there may be the like Gradations in ſeveral Tribes of Beings above me.

§ 13. As to thoſe of my own Species (from which by Analogy I may form ſome Notion of them) I find we were evidently made for Society, being furniſhed with the Power of *Speech* as well as *Reaſon*, whereby we are capable of entering into the Underſtanding of each other's Minds and Sentiments, and of holding mutual Intercourſe and Converſation one with another, and jointly conſpiring to promote our common Well-being; to which we are naturally led by a Principle of *Benevolence*, and *ſocial Diſpoſitions* and *Affections*, founded in the Frame and Condition of our Nature, which not only placeth us in the various Relations of *Huſbands* and *Wives*, *Parents* and *Children*, and other *Relatives*; but alſo lays us under a Neceſſity of mutual Dependence one upon another, which obligeth us to enter into Compacts for our Defence and Safety, and for maintaining both private Right and publick Order, and promoting the common Good of our Species, in the ſeveral Communities to which we belong. And as I have a quick Senſe of what is right in others towards me as being what I am, and of my own Eaſe and Comfort, ſo I cannot diveſt myſelf of a Senſe of what muſt, for the ſame Reaſon, be right in me towards others, and a Senſe of Tenderneſs and Compaſſion for thoſe that are in Miſery, whereby I am ſtrongly prompted to relieve them: And theſe Tendencies and Affections of *the ſocial Kind*, are evidently planted in us for promoting our ſocial Happineſs. And finally; as I cannot long enjoy myſelf in a State of Solitude, and have a ſtrong Paſſion for Society; ſo I find, in Fact, that my true Intereſt and Enjoyment of myſelf, depends on the general Intereſt and good Order of the Community, and this, in Addition to thoſe ſocial Diſpoſitions, ſtrongly prompts me to the Love of my Country, and to be forward and active in whatever may promote the publick Weal. Such are my Abilities and Advantages, and ſuch my Condition, Circumſtances and Tendencies, and thoſe of the Kind to which I ſtand related.

§ 14. But then, if I conſider myſelf a little further, I find, after all, that at beſt I am attended with very great Limitations and Imperfections. I cannot ſubſiſt myſelf a Moment in Eaſe or Exiſtence, nor add one Power or Faculty to thoſe I have: And there are certain Bounds (ſmall compared with what I can eaſily imagine) beyond which I cannot at all extend or exert them. My Sight and Hearing are very ſcanty; my Underſtanding is but ſmall; my Conceptions are very

very feeble; my Memory is very brittle; my Attention is very weak; my Knowledge is very confused; my Will is very irresolute; my Power is very infirm, and my Activity can extend but to a very small Compass.

§ 15. BUT, which is worse, I find (which is the general Complaint of every one more or less) that we are troubled with some unhappy Tendency or other, which seems to be founded in the Frame of our Nature; some idle, sensual Disposition; some importunate Appetite, or some untoward Passion, which it is very difficult to keep within reasonable Bounds, and in Indulgence to which, it is much if we have not contracted some ill Habit or other, or, at least, been guilty of many grievous Miscarriages, for which our Reason and Consciences have sadly reproached us, and given us very great Uneasiness, and sometimes terrible Apprehensions and Forebodings of Vengeance to come, unless we repent and reform. And Multitudes, I observe, are miserable Slaves to these perverse Dispositions and Habits: Hence the sad Complaints of the Prevalence of Lust, Passion, Prejudice, Pride, Deceit, Oppression, &c. much obtaining in the World, corrupting and byassing the Minds, perverting the Judgments and Resolutions of Mankind, and leading them into many Errors and Vices, to the great Mischief and Confusion of Society, as well as the Ruin of particular Persons.

§ 16. AT the same time we find, by sad Experience, that we are daily liable to many Infirmities and Diseases, Pains and Miseries, Losses and Disappointments, and perpetual Uncertainty, with respect to Life and Health, and every Thing about us, and must expect, in a little Time to quit our present State of Being, and resign to the common Fate of a Dissolution, which is called *Death*, that King of Terrors, who is incessantly making his Approaches towards us in one Shape or other. Such a strange Mixture is human Nature! Such a various Creature is Man! Such his noble Abilities and Excellencies on the one Hand, and such his Imperfections and Wretchedness on the other.

CHAP II.

Of the Author *of our* Nature, * *His* Perfections *and* Operations.

§ 1. (II.) I PROCEED now to the next Enquiry. Let every One then, in the *second* Place, seriously ask himself this Question, *How came I to be, and to be such an imperfect and sinful Being as I am?* For we cannot have a right Knowledge of ourselves, without considering, not only what we are in ourselves, but also how we stand variously related, and particularly, without looking to the Cause of our present Being and Limitations *(Introd. 26.)* and in order to answer this Question, let us consider and reason with ourselves in the following Manner.

§ 2. I KNOW that I have a Being, because I perceive and act, and that I must have had a Beginning of Existence, because there must have been a Time when I did not perceive or act, and I can

* *Quid prius dicam solitis parentis,*
Laudibus, qui res hominum ac Deorum,
Qui mare & terras, variisque mundum,
Temperat horis? HOR.

I can have no Notion of the Exiſtence of an intelligent active Being, without conſcious Perception and Activity. And if I began to be, I muſt have been made. It is certain I could not come into Being by meer *Chance*, for that is nothing but an empty Name, which we vulgarly uſe only as a Cover to our Ignorance or Inadvertence. I alſo know I did not make myſelf, for that is impoſſible, and would imply, to be, and not to be, at the ſame Time; nor have I Power to continue myſelf in Being ſo much as one Moment; nor can I a Moment ſecure my Health, or any of my Enjoyments (Part I. Chap. I. § 14.) ſo that I find I am wholly a limited and dependent Being.

§ 3. IT is therefore certain, that I muſt have had a Cauſe; for an Effect, or Thing made, without a Cauſe, is a Contradiction, and can have no Meaning: There muſt then be ſome other Being on whom I depend. And ſince *there cannot be an Effect without a Cauſe*, it is evident that the Cauſe of my Being muſt have Powers capable of producing ſuch an Effect; otherwiſe there would ſtill be an Effect without a Cauſe, than which nothing can be more abſurd. It is evident that my Parents could not be the adequate Cauſes; they could, at moſt, be only the Occaſions or Inſtruments of my Being; for it never was in their Power that I ſhould be at all, or being, that I ſhould be ſuch as I am; nor could they continue me a Moment in Being, Health or Eaſe. It is therefore plain that I muſt look higher for an adequate Cauſe, both of my Exiſtence and Subſiſtence.

§ 4. IT is moreover manifeſt, that *no Cauſe can give what it hath not*, or, which is the ſame Thing, produce an Effect more noble, or of greater Powers or Perfections than itself; for then again, there would be an Effect without a Cause, or Something produced by Nothing, which is impossible. Hence, therefore, it is plain, that what is destitute of Perception, Consciousness and Intelligence, cannot produce a perceptive, conscious, intelligent Being: What is void of any Principle of Deliberation, Liberty and Activity, cannot produce a considerate, free, active Being, *&c.* It is consequently evident, that the Being who brought me into Being, must himself be possessed of Powers or Perfections analogous to those I experience in myself.

§ 5. SINCE, therefore, I know I have some considerable Degrees of Understanding, Knowledge, Will, Force and Activity, with Freedom of Deliberation, Choice and Design, and the Powers of Self-exertion, and Self-determination, together with some Sense of Benevolence, and of Right and Wrong, or Equity and Iniquity, and some Disposition to do the one, and avoid the other (Chap. I. § 5, 6.) It is from hence evident, that the Almighty Being, who made me, and whom I call GOD, being the genuine and adequate Cause, from whom I derived, and on whom I depend, must Himself have *Understanding*, *Knowledge*, *Will*, *Force*, and *Activity*; must have *Liberty*, *Choice*, *Deliberation*, *Self-exertion*, and *Self-determination*; and must be a Being of *Equity*, *Justice* and *Goodness*, and all other moral Perfections, which are implied in these, and which are comprehended under the Terms *Holiness* and *Rectitude*. And as I am thus truly made by Him, and in some Measure to resemble Him, He must therefore be strictly and properly my *Parent*, or the *Father of my Spirit*.

§ 6. Now

§ 6. Now what I thus argue from myſelf to the Cauſe of my Exiſtence, muſt be equally true of every other intelligent active Being, that knows he muſt have had a Beginning of Exiſtence, and is limited and dependent, however ſo perfect, as well as of me. From whence it is evident, that this univerſal Cauſe muſt be poſſeſſed of the higheſt Perfections and Powers that are conceivable, or do at all obtain, and that he muſt hold them entirely independent of any other Being whatſoever: And, being independent of any other Being, it is evident, that He cannot be under the Power of any other Being to limit or controul Him, and that all other Beings muſt be entirely dependent upon Him, and conſequently muſt have derived from his Will and Power, and therefore be limited to various Degrees of Being and Perfection, as pleaſeth Him. So that He muſt hold, poſſeſs and enjoy *all poſſible Perfection* in and of Himſelf, without any poſſible *Limitation* or *Imperfection*, and muſt be the univerſal *Father of Spirits*, and was accordingly by the wiſeſt of the Ancients, ſtiled, *The Father of the Univerſe.* * του γαρ και γενος εσμεν ---χαιρε πατερ, &c. *Arat.* in St. *Paul*, *Acts* xvii. 28.

§ 7. SINCE, therefore, he thus exiſts, independent of all other Beings, and they, by the Neceſſity of their Nature, derive from Him, and depend on Him, it is plain that he muſt exiſt originally by the abſolute Neceſſity of his Nature without any Cauſe, and conſequently be *All in All*, All that truly *is*, All Perfection and Fulneſs of Being, or *Being* and Perfection, by way of Eminency, and ſo He alone muſt be the *neceſſarily exiſtent Being*, or that Being, to whom it is peculiar

* Vide *Clarke*'s and *Burnet*'s *Boyle*'s *Lectures*.

peculiar that *Existence* is necessarily implied in his very *Essence*. Hence He was, by the wisest of the Ancients, called the TO ON, and the ὁ ὄντως ὤν, or *the Being who truly exists*; and hence the Name *JEHOVAH*, by which He thought fit, from the Beginning, to be called, in Contradistinction to all precarious and dependent Beings, signifies, *The Essence existing*, or the Being whose Essence implieth Existence, and whose Existence is ever present, without any Limitation to Time or Place. †

§ 8. Nor can there be more than *One* such Being, because it is thus evident that He alone can *necessarily exist*, and that *all possible Perfections* are united in Him, or *One* in Him; it being a Contradiction, that two or more Beings should each have all possible Perfection. And since He must thus have such an absolute Fulness of Being, He is on that Account said to be *Truth* and *Good*, by way of Eminency: He is *Truth*, as in Him there is all Reality, and *Good*, as in Him there is all Excellency, even every Thing that can contribute to render both Himself and all His Creatures entirely happy; and He is called *Truth*, as He is intelligible; and *Good*, as He is eligible. He must therefore be the Source of all *Happiness*, both with regard to the *Intellect*, *Will*, *Affections* and *Activity*.

§ 9. In this Method of Reasoning it is evident, that the great Cause or Author of my Being and Powers, and those of all other Spirits, or intelligent active Beings, must necessarily be *Infinite*, *Eternal* and *Unchangeable*. For if He be out of the Power of every other Being to limit or controul Him, his Knowledge, Power and Activity, cannot be confined to any particular Object,

† Vide *Hutchinson*'s *Moses Sine Principio*.

Object, in any Point of Space or Duration, since all Being, Time and Place, depend on Him, nor can He be liable to any Change from any Power whatsoever, since all Powers derive from Him. So that, as there never was a Time when He could have begun to be, so it is impossible he should ever cease to be, or be altered from what he is. And for the same Reason that he cannot but be present here or there, or to every particular Person or Thing, in any assignable Place or Point of Space, he cannot but be every where else, or *Omnipresent*, since all Existence perpetually depends on Him. And hence it is plain, that all Things past, present, or to come, in all Parts of the Universe, must at once be present to Him, as being perfectly known to Him, and subject to Him, as being intirely dependent on his Almighty Will and Power.

§ 10. NOR can I doubt of the Existence of such a *necessary and eternal* Being, from the Existence of *necessary and eternal Truth.* There are a great Number of evident Truths that come within our Reach, which I find exist necessarily and eternally independent of my Mind, or any other created Mind whatsoever, by the Light and Evidence of many of which (to which I find my Mind is passive) I am enabled to judge of True and False, and of Right and Wrong, in every particular Case: Such as these, *Action implies Existence*; *an Effect must suppose a Cause*; the Whole *is bigger than either of its Parts*; *Things equal to another are equal among themselves*; *what is Right or Wrong in another towards me, must be equally Right or Wrong in me towards him*, &c. Now, these and the like Truths imply the necessary Habitudes of certain Essences that do not depend on any particular Existences in Nature, and must therefore

therefore have an antecedent mental or intellectual Existence; and there can be no Conception of Truth without a Mind perceiving it, or in which it exists. Since, therefore, there are eternal Truths necessarily existing, independent of any created Mind, or any Thing existing in Nature, it is evident there must be an eternal, necessarily existing, independent Mind, in which they originally exist, as one eternal Light of Truth, and by whom they are exhibited to all other Minds in various Measures, according to their several Capacities and Application, enabling them to judge of every particular Thing that comes within their Notice. * He is therefore the great *Parent Mind*, from whom derives all Light and Knowledge to every created Intelligence, being, as it were, the intellectual Sun enlightening our Minds, as the sensible Sun, by his incessant Activity, enlighteneth our Eyes.

§ 11. WHAT I have thus argued from my own Existence, Powers and Faculties, and those of every other intelligent and active Creature, and from the Existence of eternal Truth, may be also demonstrated from the Existence of every sensible Thing that I see, hear and feel, from without me. I know that I am not the Cause of any of those Impressions that are made upon my Senses; Light, Colours, Sounds, tangible Qualities, *&c.* I am sure they do not depend upon my Will and Activity; for I am intirely passive in the Reception of them. Nor can they be without a Cause, nor yet from any senseless, inert or unactive Cause, for that is a Contradiction in Terms. They must therefore be

* Vide *Norris*'s Ideal World and Miscellanies, and *Cambray*'s Demonstration.

be the conſtant Effects of an intelligent Cauſe, intimately preſent with me, and inceſſantly active upon me, who continually produceth all theſe Senſations in my Mind, correſpondent to the Archetypes in his all-comprehending Intellect, according to certain ſtable Laws, or fixed Rules, which He hath eſtabliſhed to Himſelf, and which are commonly called the Laws of Nature. When therefore I conſider the whole Syſtem of theſe ſenſible, as well as the intelligible, Objects that ſurround me, and under the Impreſſion of which I continually live, I muſt conclude, that *I live, and move, and have my Being*, in Him, who is the perpetual and *Almighty* Author of them. *

§ 12. I FIND theſe ſenſible Objects are all firmly connected together, Things viſible with Things tangible, and all the various Combinations of them one with another, ſo as to conſtitute one moſt beautiful and uſeful Whole, which we call the *natural World*; in all which I do manifeſtly diſcern the moſt wiſe Deſign, and the moſt exquiſite Contrivance and Adjuſtment of Ends and Means (Chap. I. § 10.) from whence I gather, that they muſt be the Effects of a moſt wiſe and deſigning Cauſe. And I do evidently experience that they are all contrived in the beſt Manner to render them ſubſervient to all the Purpoſes of my Subſiſtence and Well-being, and that of the whole rational and moral Syſtem, which we call the *Moral World*; from whence I muſt conclude the glorious Author of them to be, not only an infinitely *wiſe* and *powerful*, but moreover an infinitely *kind* and *benevolent* Being.

§ 13. I DO not, indeed, find, upon a cloſe Examination, that there is any neceſſary Connection

* Vide Biſhop *Berkeley*'s Dialogues, Pages 78, 79, &c.

tion between them; for Instance, between the Objects of *Sight* and *Feeling*; the one appears to have only the Nature of a Sign with Regard to the other, being all alike, meer passive Perceptions in our Minds, between which there can be no Relation of Causality: So that the Connection between them, tho' stable, is entirely arbitrary; as is that between the Sound, *Man*, and the Thing signified by it: From whence I gather, that I must unavoidably consider the one with regard to the other, to have the Nature of a wonderful Language,* whereby the great Author of Nature appears to be continually present with me, discovering his Mind and Will to me (and that in a stable and invariable Manner, which I find I can always depend upon) and, as it were, speaking to me, and directing me how to act, and conduct myself in all the Affairs of Life; whereby he manifestly discovereth a constant watchful *Providence* over me in all my Ways. From whence it is evident, not only that He is, but that He must be, both a Being of infinite *Goodness*, *Wisdom* and *Power*, and of the most stable *Truth*, and invariable *Integrity*.

§ 14. I do moreover see and feel a vast Variety of *Motions*, on the Laws of which, most wisely contrived, dependeth the whole Order, Harmony and Usefulness of the natural World. But it is certain that nothing corporeal can move itself, being, as such, meerly passive and inert; and yet it is no less evident, that Motion implies Force and Activity in the Mover; † and since nothing can act where it is not, it manifestly follows, that in all the wisely contrived Motions of

* Vide *Minute Philosopher*, Dial. 4.

† *Mens agitat molem.* VIRG.

of Nature, as well as all other Objects of Senſe, both in the Heavens above, and in the Earth below, we conſtantly ſee and feel the univerſal Preſence of that moſt *wiſely deſigning*, and moſt *powerfully active*, *all-comprehending Mind*, who both begins and continues Motion, and is therefore the *Almighty Author* and *Preſerver* of all Things.

§ 15. I SAY, we both *ſee and feel his univerſal Preſence*; for it is manifeſt, that He may as truly be ſaid to be an Object of Senſe as any human Perſon; for, What do I ſee when I behold a King? Not the Spirit or Soul, which is properly the Perſon, and which, in the Nature of it, cannot be an Object of Senſe; I ſee only the Shape and Colour of a Man, cloathed with gorgeous Robes. In like Manner, I cannot ſee GOD, as He is a Spirit, and, as ſuch, is inviſible; but I as truly ſee Him, as I ſee a Man like myſelf; nay, indeed, more manifeſtly than I can behold any mortal Man; for I ſee Him in every viſible Shape and Form in all Nature; I behold Him in all the infinitely various Modifications of *Light* and Colours throughout the whole Creation; in all which, He is every where preſent, being, as it were, *cloathed with Light, as with a Garment*; which Expreſſion is rightly obſerved to be of like Import with that Saying of the ancient Eaſtern Sages, That *GOD hath Light for his Body, and Truth for his Soul.* * In the ſame Manner, I may truly ſay, I feel Him in the *Heat* and Wind, and in every tangible Figure and Motion, *&c.* I hear Him in every Sound, and taſte Him in every Morſel, *&c.* In a Word, I muſt again ſay, it is He who is *All in All*.

§ 16 FUR-

* Vide *Minute Philoſopher*, Dial. 4. § 5, and 15.

§ 16. FURTHERMORE (not to descend to that infinite World of minute Creatures, which the Microscope opens to our View, and which gives us surprising Apprehensions of the DEITY) as I observe all these sensible Objects about me, are connected together, in a wonderful Manner, into one most beautiful and useful System, and made subservient to my Subsistence and Well-being, and those of my Species, in this Mansion allotted to us; so I observe this Globe, on which we live, to be no less wonderfully connected with the *Sun* and other *Planets*, with us surrounding and depending on him, so that they all make one entire System; the other Globes being probably design'd for Uses analagous to this of ours. And as the prodigious Number of *fixed Stars* seem to be of the same Nature, so it is probable they are designed for the like Purposes with those for which I find our *Sun*, the great Source of *Light* and *Life* to us, is manifestly fitted and designed, and consequently may have Globes like ours, depending on them. If so, as this gives me a stupendous Idea of the vast Extent and Variety of the mighty Works of GOD, so it must give me astonishing Apprehensions of His excellent *Greatness*, *Majesty* and *Glory*, who must be equally present with them all, and does alike display his infinite *Wisdom*, *Power* and *Goodness* in them, to all the admiring Beholders; having His whole vast *Family of Heaven and Earth*, alike depending upon Him, and deriving their All from Him, *in all Places of His Dominion*.

§ 17. WHAT is thus evident to me from the *Frame and Constitution* of the *natural World*, is no less evident from the *Constitution* of the *moral World*. For, as I see all the *Order*, *Harmony* and *Use-*

Uſefulneſs of Nature depends on the Laws of (what is called) *Attraction*, by which the vaſt Globes keep their Situations, and proceed inceſſantly in their perpetual Rounds, and all the Parts and Appendages of each Globe are firmly kept together; and alſo on the ſurprizing *Inſtincts* by which the ſeveral Tribes of Animals are led to provide for their Subſiſtence, and the Continuance of their Species, which can no otherwiſe be accounted for, than from the meer paſſive Impreſſions of the great Almighty Mind, that ſubſiſts and governs the World in the beſt and wiſeſt Manner: So I obſerve all the Order, Harmony and Happineſs of the *moral World*, depends on the Laws of *Benevolence* (Chap. I. § 13.) which taking its Riſe in the natural Affection between the Sexes, Parents, Children, and other Relatives, ſpreads through the whole Species, ſtrongly attaching them to ſocial Life; which ſtrong Tendency of *Benevolence* in the *moral World*, is plainly analogous to *Attraction* and *Inſtincts* in the *natural*, and muſt accordingly be a like paſſive Impreſſion of the ſame great Parent-governing Mind, who plainly deſigns hereby to keep the moral World together, and in order; and by Him alſo it is manifeſt, that all created Minds are paſſively enlightened, to have a quick Senſe, and intuitive Evidence of the Fit, the Fair, and Decent in Behaviour (*Introd.* 15. And Chap. II. § 10.) and thence, the Laws by which this Principle of Benevolence muſt be regulated, in order to their univerſal Harmony and Happineſs. From hence, therefore, alſo evidently appears, not only His *Exiſtence*, *Omnipreſence*, and infinite *Wiſdom* and *Power*, but alſo his infinite *Benevolence* and *Equity*, befitting the Character of Him, who is the great *Father* and *Lord of the Universe*.

§ 18. Now it being evident from all that hath been said, that this glorious Being, whom I call my GOD, must be a Being of all possible Perfection; it is plain that He must have an intire and absolute *Sufficiency* in and of Himself to His own Happiness, and therefore cannot need any of His Creatures, or any Thing they can do to make Him happy, nor can any Thing they can do, make Him otherwise. And from His absolute *Independency*, and their continual and intire Dependence upon His Will and Power (§ 6.) I must conclude, that He is not only the *Almighty Creator* and *most high Possessor* of *Heaven and Earth*, and of every Creature therein; but, moreover, that He is the continual *Preserver* of all His Creatures, and consequently, that the Moment He should cease to will the Continuance of their Existence, they must unavoidably cease, and drop into nothing.

§ 19. Nor can it, I think, be conceived, that the infinitely wise, powerful, just and good Author of my Being, and of all other intelligent active Creatures, would neglect us, and take no further Care of us. I cannot imagine, from His Attributes above demonstrated, but that He must look after each of His Creatures, and see what use we make of the Being, Powers and Advantages He hath given us, and take Care to instruct and conduct us to the End He designed, and that in a Manner suitable to the Nature and Powers which He hath given us (Chap. I. § 2, 5.) It cannot therefore be, but that, as he evidently governs the *natural World*, in a passive Manner, suitable to its passive Nature, by the Laws which He

He hath eſtabliſhed to Himſelf (being Himſelf, properly ſpeaking, the ſole Agent) ſo He muſt much more govern the *moral World* (as being in itſelf of vaſtly the greateſt Worth, and the End of the other) in a Manner ſuitable to its rational and moral Nature, to whom He hath given to be a Syſtem of intelligent, conſcious, free Agents, and conſequently capable of *moral Government*, by Laws and Motives, ſuggeſted to their Reaſon and Conſciences, and to their Hopes and Fears: And conſequently I cannot doubt but I am ſubject to His Conduct and Government, and that he will thus govern me as a reaſonable and moral Agent; and that, in Conſequence of this, He will call me to an Account, and ſee how I ſhall have conducted myſelf in this State of Probation, in the Uſe of the Abilities and Talents which he hath committed to my Truſt, and judge whether I have endeavoured to anſwer the End of my Being, in Conformity to the Laws of that reaſonable and Self-active Nature, which he hath given me, and make me fare well or ill, according as my Behaviour ſhall be found to have been good or bad. That this is fit and reaſonable to be expected, my own Conſcience ſtrongly ſuggeſts (Chap. I. § 11, 15.) and that Happineſs or Miſery, will be the Effect of Virtue or Vice, the Nature of the Things themſelves loudly proclaims (it being a no leſs evident Law of Nature in Morals, than in Naturals, That *whatſoever a Man ſoweth, that ſhall he alſo reap.**) Nor can it be doubted but that He, who is Holineſs and Righteouſneſs itſelf, cannot but love thoſe Qualities wherever He beholds them, and muſt therefore be engaged to make them happy; nor can His Juſtice fail to

* Vide *Turnbull*, Vol. 2.

make the contrary miserable. So that as sure as He is *just* and *good*, so sure He will *reward* the one, and *punish* the other. And what is thus reasonable to think with regard to myself, must be equally true with regard to all other intelligent Creatures. GOD must therefore be, not only the *Almighty Creator* and *Preserver*, but also the *supreme Ruler*, and *moral Governor* of the World; the great *King*, *Lord* and *Judge* of the whole Universe, which therefore is His *Kingdom*, in which He most wisely and uncontroulably presides, and orders all Things for the Good of the Whole, in a Manner suitable to the best Interest of each Nature. I cannot therefore doubt but that He will in the Whole and Result of Things, bring Good out of Evil, and make Evil itself subservient to Good, and even over-rule the Sins and Follies of His Creatures, so as finally to answer the best Ends.

§ 20. If now it be enquired, *How I came to be such an imperfect, frail, sinful Being, as I am?* Or how it could be, that the wise and good God that made me, who is Himself the most perfect and best of Beings, should make me such an imperfect, sinful and miserable Creature, as I find myself to be? (Chap. I. § 15.) To this I must answer in the following Manner: That GOD should make me such an imperfect (or less perfect) Creature as I am, compared with others, or with what I can easily imagine, I see no Reason to doubt; inasmuch as my Being itself, and every Perfection of it, and Advantage attending it, must be His sovereign free Gift, and what He was in no wise obliged to bestow. He is the sovereign Lord of His Favours, and must therefore be intirely at Liberty to bestow such De-

grees

grees of Being and Perfection, and ſuch Advantages, greater or leſs, as He thinks fit; and it appears that He hath delighted in a boundleſs Variety in all His Works.

§ 21. INDEED that He ſhould, without any known voluntary Fault of mine, put me into a Condition that is, in the Whole, worſe than not to be; or that He ſhould, in giving me my Being, lay me under an abſolute Neceſſity of being finally ſinful and miſerable; this would be a very hard Caſe indeed: But this I muſt think utterly impoſſible, as being what I cannot think conſiſtent with His Wiſdom, Holineſs, Juſtice and Goodneſs, above demonſtrated.* But ſo long as I have ſuch a Being as is deſirable, tho' attended with great Frailties, Limitations and Imperfections, and am put into ſuch a Condition as renders me capable of further Improvements, and of attaining to ſome good Degree of Happineſs, if I am not wanting to myſelf, and ſince I ſhall not be obliged to account for any more than I have received; I cannot reaſonably complain, but ought to be very thankful for it, tho' I ſee others have much greater Advantages than I, from whom, in all Reaſon, a proportionably greater Account will be expected.

§ 22. AND as to my being ſo *ſinful* a Creature as I muſt confeſs I am, this I cannot aſcribe to GOD; for ſince the formal Notion of *Sin* conſiſts in the voluntary Oppoſition of our Wills to the known Will of GOD, or the Conſtitution which He hath made, it muſt be the Fault of my Will, and not of His; and accordingly my own Conſcience tells me, whenever I do amiſs, that I myſelf (and not He) am the

 Cauſe,

* Vide *Wollaſt. R. N.* Page 200.

Cause, and true Author of all the Wickedness I commit. If, therefore, instead of being obedient to the Author of my Being, and making a good Use of my Liberty, and of the Powers and Advantages He hath given me, and thereby further improving them, and qualifying myself for the Happiness He designs for me in so doing, I make a bad Use of them, by voluntarily acting contrary to His known Will, and thereby sink myself into a worse Condition; nay, tho' it were into a worse Condition than not to be, it is wholly owing to myself, and not to Him that made me.

§ 23. If now I should ask, Why hath GOD made me at all peccable, or capable of Sin? This would be the same as to ask, Why hath He made me capable of Duty? Or, why hath He made me a free Agent? But this would be a strange Question; for without Liberty I should be destitute of one of the chief Excellencies of my rational Nature, and should not be capable of either Duty or Sin, properly speaking; for as Sin consists in a free and voluntary Disobedience, so Duty consists in a free and willing Obedience to the known Will of GOD. So that without a Power of Liberty or free Agency, there could have been no such Thing as either Virtue or Vice, Praise or Blame; nor can either the one or the other obtain, but in Proportion to the Knowledge we have, or may have, of what we ought to do, and the Powers we are furnished with, either to do or forbear. *

§ 24. And, lastly, as to the many Pains, Calamities and Dissolution, to which I am liable (Chap. I. § 16.) I must think, that as I am a Sinner, I need a Course of Discipline: That it is fit

* Vide *Wollast. R. N.* Page 62.

fit natural Evil ſhould attend moral Evil, as the beſt Means for the Cure of it: And that therefore GOD, having it in View that we would abuſe our Liberty, not only juſtly, but wiſely and kindly ordered theſe Calamities, as being the fitteſt Means that could have been uſed to bring us to Repentance and Reformation, and to diſcipline us to Virtue, by mortifying our Luſts, and diſengaging us from thoſe Objects that are moſt apt to enſnare and miſlead us; and, at the ſame time, they give us Occaſion and Opportunity for the Exerciſe of ſeveral Virtues of very great Uſe towards the perfecting our reaſonable and active Nature, which otherwiſe could have had no Place; and ſince we cannot, as Things now are, be completely happy here, they lead us to the Hopes of a better State hereafter.

§ 25. THUS it appears to me, that, without any Imputation upon either the Wiſdom, Power, Juſtice or Goodneſs of GOD, we may ſufficiently account for all the Sin and Calamity that obtain in the World. But if, after all, there ſhould be ſome untoward Appearances in the Conduct of Providence that we cannot clearly account for, they ought not to be admitted as any juſt Objections againſt what hath been antecedently demonſtrated; eſpecially ſince we ſhould be very vain indeed, to think ourſelves qualified to be competent Judges of *the deep Things of GOD*. We ſee but a ſmall Part, a very ſhort Scene of the vaſt *Drama*, and therefore are not able to make any tolerable Judgment of the Whole: So that what to us may have the Appearance of Evil, may, in the whole, have the Nature of Good; and it becometh us, for that Reaſon, to have an implicit Faith in the infinite Wiſdom, Power,

Justice and Goodness of the Deity, above demonstrated, that it will prove so in the Whole and Result of Things. And that this Expectation may appear the more reasonable, I proceed now to the next Enquiry.

CHAP III.

Of the End *of our* Being, *and of our* future State.

§ 1. (III.) LET every one then, in the *third* Place, seriously consider further, and enquire with Himself, *For what End was I thus brought into Being, and am thus continually subsisted by Almighty GOD?* And for the Resolution of this Question, let him thus think and reason with himself, or to this Effect:

§ 2. THAT I was not made at all Adventures, without any Contrivance and Design, but must have been made for some End or other, I cannot doubt, since I have evidently found, that He who gave me my Being, must Himself be a Being of all possible Perfections, and consequently must be a most kind, wise and designing Cause; especially since I do also evidently find in Fact, so many, and such manifest Tokens of the wisest and most benevolent Design and Contrivance in my whole Frame, and in every Thing about me (Chap. I. § 2, 9, 10.)

§ 3. BEING therefore made by a most wise and good Cause, I must necessarily have been made for some wise and good End. And having demonstrated that the Being who made me, hath an an infinite Sufficiency within Himself for His own Happiness, independent of any other Being (Chap. II. § 18.) it is manifest that whatever good End He had in giving me my Being, it could not be to serve Himself of me, or to promote any Advantage to Himself by me: This were a Thought infinitely too mean to entertain of Him, who is *GOD*, *All-sufficient*, that it could be possible for Him to stand in need of me, or of any Thing I could do or suffer, in order to His own Happiness.

§ 4. MOREOVER, since it hath been evidently discovered that the Author of my Being is infinitely perfect, and consequently perfectly just and good; perfectly equitable and benevolent (Chap. II. § 6, 17.) it is evident that He could not give me my Being with any malevolent Design, or with a Design that I should be absolutely and unavoidably miserable in the Whole; nor could He (as I humbly conceive) design Misery for me, or any of His Creatures, but in Consequence of their personal, voluntary Demerit, by persisting in wilful Rebellion against Him, or the general Interest of the Constitution which He hath made; for this would be so far from consisting with Equity and Benevolence, that it would imply the very Notion of Cruelty. A Thought which we should remove at an infinite Distance from that most perfect and best of Beings.

§ 5. INDEED, in case of wilful Rebellion, finally persisted in, it is fit and right, and even necessary for the Good of the Whole (being the most effectual Means to cure Rebellion, and secure the Obedience of GOD's Creatures, which is necessary for their general Good and Happiness) that Punishment should be inflicted upon those

that

that rebel, and obſtinately oppoſe their Wills to the Conſtitution He hath made, and the Ends of His Government, in Proportion to their ſeveral Crimes and Miſdemeanors (Chap. II. § 19.) And indeed Miſchief and Miſery do, in the Nature of Things, neceſſarily reſult from Sin and Vice. But it cannot be therefore ſuppoſed that their Miſery could be His primary Deſign, or that He ſhould intend their Rebellion, or lay them under a Neceſſity of Sinning, that they might be finally miſerable; for this would, in Effect, be abſolutely to deſign their Miſery, and delight in it as ſuch, which to Him muſt be infinitely impoſſible.

§ 6. On the contrary, ſince GOD is evidently a moſt kind and benevolent Being, and could therefore have no other than kind and benevolent Ends, in giving Being to His rational Creatures, it is plain that His primary Intention muſt have been ſo far from that of making them to be miſerable, that He did undoubtedly make them with a Deſign that they might be, in ſome good Degree, happy, in the Participation and Enjoyment of His Goodneſs, in Proportion to their ſeveral Capacities and Qualifications. And that this was, in Fact, His End, is alſo manifeſt from the Frame and Structure of the Nature which He hath given them; for He hath given them Conſciouſneſs, whereby they are capable of Self-enjoyment; Intelligence, whereby they are able to conſider and judge of what is fit and needful to the Enjoyment of themſelves; Paſſions, whereby they are prompted to deſire and endeavour what contributes to their Well-being, and to guard and defend themſelves againſt what may be hurtful to them; and a Principle of Activity, to procure the one, and avoid the other; and of Liberty, whereby they are able to ſuſpend Judging

ing and Acting, till they can duly ballance their Passions, and act with Advantage. And besides these Powers, which are Means to their personal Happiness, He hath also inspired them with social Affections, which render them capable of social Happiness: Having therefore given them the Means, it is plain He must have designed the End. (Chap. I. § 5, 7, 13.)

§ 7. THIS then being the Frame of that Nature, which GOD hath given us, it must plainly be His Design that we should seek our Happiness, in affecting and acting conformable to it; otherwise, if we act inconsistent with ourselves, and so do a Violence to our own Nature; in this Case, we can neither enjoy ourselves, nor any Thing else, and so must be unavoidably miserable. Inasmuch therefore as GOD hath made us to be intelligent, free, active Creatures; and since our Happiness must immediately depend upon the right Use of these Powers, and must consist in the free and vigorous Exertion of them, in Conformity to the great Law of our Nature, which is the inward Sense of our own Reason and Consciences; it must accordingly be His Design, not only that we should be happy, but that we should be so by Means of our own Activity, and by our always freely acting reasonably, and consequently that we should cultivate and improve our Reason in the best Manner we can, under the Circumstances in which He hath placed us, in order to make a right Judgment how we ought to affect and act, and conduct ourselves to the best Advantage for our own Happiness.

§ 8. IT may, indeed, be truly said, that *GOD made all Things for His own Glory*, if it be rightly understood. But wherein then doth His Glory consist? It is plain, it cannot consist in the Disorder,

der, Confusion and Misery, of His Creatures; nor can it consist meerly in being applauded by them. It is, indeed, fit and right in itself, and for our Good, as well as His Honour, and therefore He requireth it, that we should daily acknowledge Him to be what He is, our Creator, Preserver and Benefactor; and all that is fit and right, fair and decent, true and good, must, as such, be His Glory, as being in itself conformable to His infinitely perfect Intellect and Will, as well as beatifying to His Creatures; and accordingly nothing can be of greater Use and Advantage to us, than that we live under a deep and habitual Sense of this. But it would be a most unworthy Thought of Him, to imagine that he made us for the Sake of being applauded, or that He requireth even these just Acknowledgments for His own Sake, as though we, or our Services, could be any Advantage to Him. This would be to make Him a most selfish Being indeed; especially if we should imagine that He could aim at Applause or Glory, at the Expence of our unavoidable and endless Misery: This would be a most dishonourable and shocking Thought.

§ 9. So far from this, that I must conceive it to be the Glory of GOD to communicate His Perfections in various Degrees, so far as they are communicable, and to display His Goodness to His Creatures, and make them happy in the Participation of it, in Proportion to their several Capacities, and this in Consequence of their acting in Obedience to Him, and in Conformity to His Law, which is the Law of their Natures. For since He was pleased to give them their Being, it cannot be but that, as the tender Father of His own Off-spring, He will account it His Interest

tereſt and Glory to ſee them as happy as may be, conſiſtent with the Intereſt of the whole Family (to which it is fit every Individual ſhould reſign) and take Pleaſure in every Thing that contributes to their Happineſs, and abhor whatſoever is deſtructive to it, and inconſiſtent with it, as His greateſt Diſhonour.

§ 10. FOR ſince He that wills the End, muſt will the Means neceſſary to that End, it is plain that ſince GOD wills our Happineſs in the Whole, as our End, and his Glory, it muſt be his Will and Law concerning us, that we avoid every Thing that doth, in the Nature of it, tend to make us miſerable, and that we do every Thing that doth, in the Nature of it, tend to make us happy (*Introd.* 23.) So that the Glory of GOD, and our Happineſs, with the Means neceſſary to it, and his Diſhonour, and our Miſery, with the Means which tend to that, muſt neceſſarily be coincident, and come in Effect to one and the ſame Thing.

§ 11. AND ſince it is evident, from Experience, that Sin and Vice doth, in the Nature of it, tend to make us miſerable; being contrary to to all that is reaſonable and right; contrary to the Attributes and Will of GOD; contrary to the clear Senſe of our own Minds, and to all the Intereſts of Society; and muſt therefore do a perpetual Violence to our reaſonable and ſocial Nature; and conſequently be moſt odious in the Sight of GOD, and all intelligent Beings, as being unavoidably attended with Horror and Confuſion, both perſonal and ſocial: And ſince, on the other Hand, it is no leſs evident, that a virtuous and dutiful Temper and Behaviour, doth, in the Nature of it, tend to our Happineſs

pineſs, becauſe it conſiſteth in doing all that is reaſonable and right, all that is agreeable to the Attributes and Will of GOD, to the Senſe of our own Minds, and to all the Intereſts of Society, and therefore muſt neceſſarily approve itſelf, as moſt beautiful and amiable in the Sight of GOD, and all reaſonable Beings, as being attended with univerſal Harmony, Peace and Joy, both within and without, with regard both to GOD and Man; it is hence evident, that GOD's Glory muſt conſiſt in our purſuing our own Happineſs, by avoiding the one, and doing the other.

§ 12. BUT now to return: Since I am convinced, from the above Method of Reaſoning, that my Well-being and Happineſs muſt have been GOD's End in giving me my Being, and that it muſt be a Happineſs ſuitable to that Nature which He hath given me, in the Whole of it; I muſt be perſuaded, that ſince, beſides an animal and ſenſitive, He hath moreover given me a rational, active and ſocial Nature, as my ſuperior and peculiar Character (Chap. I. § 5.) it is plain He muſt have deſigned me, not meerly for a ſenſual and animal, but chiefly for a rational, active and ſocial Happineſs.

§ 13. IT cannot therefore be ſuppoſed an End worthy of GOD, and agreeable to the Nature He hath given me, in the Whole of it, that I ſhould have been brought into Being, only to eat and drink, and ſleep, and enjoy the empty Gratifications of the animal Life, and that my Reaſon, and other ſuperior Powers, ſhould be deſigned only to be ſubſervient to theſe inferior Pleaſures (and in Effect only to render me more a Beaſt than I ſhould have been without them) and that after a few Days ſpent in theſe low, grovelling Purſuits and Enjoyments, I ſhould then

then be utterly extinct, ceafe, and be no more. Thefe fhort lived animal Enjoyments are indeed Ends fuitable to the Nature of a meer Beaft, and for which he is better qualified than I am: But if thefe could be fuppofed all the Ends that I was made for, the noble Powers of Reafon, Reflection, Self-exertion and Self-determination, muft have been given me in vain; nay, indeed to the worft Purpofes, as they only ferve to make me more exquifitely fenfual, and, at the fame time, fenfible of my Wretchednefs.

§ 14. AT leaft this is certain, that thefe noble Powers render me capable of a vaftly higher End, and nobler Happinefs, and which cannot attain to its Perfection here: For when I confider the wretched Circumftances of my Condition in this Life, it is plain that fuch a Happinefs can be but a little While, and but very imperfectly enjoyed, in this prefent, fhort, uncertain and uneafy State, amidft fo many Sins and Follies, Embarrafments and Perplexities, as I am, at beft, unavoidably attended with, while in this Body. Since therefore I am evidently made for fuch an Happinefs, and that it cannot attain to any tolerable Degree of Perfection here, I muft conclude that my Exiftence fhall undoubtedly reach beyond this fhort and uncertain Life, and extend forward to endlefs Ages. Without this Conclufion, I cannot fee how I fhall ever attain to any End worthy of the Wifdom and Goodnefs of the GOD that made me, and fuitable to the fuperior Nature and Powers which he hath given me, and the fuperior Happinefs I am evidently capable of.

§ 15. AND that I may live on, notwithftanding what is vulgarly called *Death*, and am of a Nature

Nature capable of proceeding on to a nobler and more perfect Kind of Life, I cannot doubt, when I consider the vastly different Natures of Spirit and Body, of which I consist (the one in itself perceptive, conscious and Self-active, the other of itself meerly senseless, inert and passive) so intirely different, that I cannot conceive of any Thing common to them, besides bare Existence, or of any natural or necessary Connection between them: I can conceive of no other than a meer arbitrary Connection, depending only on the Laws of their Union, which, in Natures so different, can, I think, be no other than the meer arbitrary Will of the Deity, and His perpetual *Fiat*. The Soul, therefore, being of a Nature intirely different from that of the Body, cannot be capable of any corporeal Laws and Affections, and consequently cannot be liable to any such Change or Dissolution as Bodies are; *i. e.* being a perceptive, active, simple, unextended, indivisible Substance, it must be naturally indiscerpible, and consequently incorruptible. I cannot therefore imagine how the Dissolution of the Body should affect the Existence of the Soul, any more than the putting off an old Garment, to put on a new One, should affect the Existence of the Body. So that I cannot consider my Body as being *myself*, or, indeed, as being properly any Part of *myself*; my Soul or Mind, that intelligent active Principle, and that only, being properly *myself*; and my Body I can only consider as a Machine to which I am at present confined, and an Engine or Organ which I am obliged to make use of, in my various Perceptions and Exertions, *ad extra*. (Chap. I. § 8, 9.) * § 16. In-

* Συ ει ἡ Ψυχη, το δε Σωμα σου, τα δε εκτος του Σωματος. Vide *Hierocles* in *Pyth. Car. Au.* & *Socrat.* in *Plato de Animo.*

§ 16. INASMUCH, therefore, as I am a Spirit of an incorruptible Nature, and know that I have Powers capable of the ſublime and noble Pleaſures of Contemplation and Virtue, which yet cannot, in any Meaſure, attain to their Perfection here, I muſt believe, that, if I am not wanting to myſelf, they ſhall attain to it hereafter. I can, indeed, with much Labour and Struggle, make ſome little Proficiency in them in my preſent State: But when I have done ſo, and am capable and earneſtly deſirous of proceeding further, muſt I ceaſe, and be no more? Can it be thought that the tender *Father of my Spirit*, would, after all my Pains, drop me into Nothing, and at once fuſtrate all my Hopes and Labours? Can there, in this Caſe, any wiſe and good Reaſons be conceived for putting an End to my Being and my Hopes together? On the contrary, would not this ſeem extremely hard and unreaſonable, and conſequently utterly inconſiſtent, and not of a Piece, with the Conduct of Him, who muſt be a Being perfectly reaſonable and equitable.

§ 17. I DO moreover find within myſelf a Fore-boding of ſomething to come after this Life, which I cannot get rid of, and an eager Appetite and earneſt Aſpiration after Immortality, that I may be capable of an endleſs Enjoyment of thoſe noble and immortal Pleaſures, which I cannot diſengage myſelf from; nor can I think any One, capable of ſerious Conſideration, can be diſengaged from theſe Views, at leaſt till he has contracted ſo much Guilt as to wiſh he may go out of Being, and is ſo immerſed in Senſuality, as to have loſt Sight of them, and be totally diſaffected to them, ſo as to become a meer

Brute of the worſt Sort, a Kind of rational Brute, and ſo a Monſter. Now I do not find any natural Appetite, as this evidently is (Chap. I. § 8.) no, not of the meaneſt Kind, nor in the moſt deſpicable Creature, but that GOD hath provided a ſuitable Object correſpondent to it; can it then be imagined that he would create ſuch a noble Appetite in ſo noble a Creature as Man, and have provided no Object ſuitable and correſpondent to that? It cannot be.

§ 18. THIS Reaſoning is abundantly confirmed to be right, when I conſider further, * that in my preſent Situation, a long and laborious Courſe of ſtedfaſt Perſiſting in the Cauſe of Truth and Virtue, in ſpite of the ſtrongeſt Solicitations to the contrary, is in this World many Times contemned, diſregarded, derided, and even barbarouſly treated and oppreſſed, without any Redreſs, and perſecuted even to Death itſelf, and ſometimes to the moſt barbarous Deaths; and that as long a Courſe of unreſtrained Indulgence to the vileſt and moſt miſchievous Vices, is frequently attended with uninterrupted Proſperity to the very laſt; I cannot therefore doubt, from the Wiſdom, Power, Holineſs, Juſtice and Goodneſs of GOD, but that the Time muſt come, when He will bring Good out of all this Evil, and theſe *crooked Things ſhall be made ſtraight*; and that He who cannot but love Virtue, as being His own Likeneſs, will reward it, and make it, in the Whole, eventually happy, even above and beyond its natural Tendency: And that He who cannot but hate Vice, as being contrary to His Nature, will eventually puniſh it with due Severity,

* See this Argument finiſhed in the beſt Manner by Mr. *Wollaſton*, in *Rel. N.* Pages 200, 210.

Severity, and make it very miserable; which indeed it cannot but be in the Nature of the Thing itself. (Chap. II. § 19.)

§ 19. THE chief Difficulty that lies in the Way of this Persuasion of a future State, is the Inconceivableness of it: But this, I think, can be no reasonable Objection against it: For who, that had never seen any Thing but the universal Desolation and Death of a severe Winter, could conceive any Thing of the exquisite Beauties and admirable Productions of a fine Spring and Summer? Indeed I can no more conceive how my Soul is now united to my Body, and perceives and acts by Means of it, and by a meer Thought can move its unweildy Limbs at Pleasure, than I can conceive how it can exist, perceive and act, after what we call Death, without this gross tangible Machine, to which it is at present confined. I can, however, a little assist my Imagination in forming some glimmering Notion of that future State, from this easy Supposition of a Man born blind and deaf, who, at the same time, hath the Senses of Feeling, Tasting and Smelling.* Now, to this Man, the tangible World, with the various Objects of Taste and Smell, is all the World that he can have any Notion of, any more than I can conceive of those *Things which Eye hath not seen, nor Ear heard, nor have they enter'd into the Heart of Man to conceive.* I, who have the visible World about me, and the Perception of various Sounds, am to this Man, what I may suppose Angels and other Spirits are to me: He can no more conceive of the visible World that I converse with, than I can conceive of the spiritual World, or the fu-

* *Guardian*, No. 27.

ture State of my Being. Now, let me only conceive this Man to be deprived of the Senſes of Feeling, Taſting and Smelling, and he is dead, intirely dead, to all the World that he had ever any Notion of. But then imagine his Eyes and Ears to be opened, and to have this glorious Show of viſible Objects, Light and Colours, with all their various Modifications, ſet before him, with a no leſs wonderful Variety of harmonious Sounds; I muſt conceive him to have intirely a new World open upon him, to which he was before an utter Stranger. He is indeed dead to the dark tangible World, but he hath exchanged it for a new viſible World. Such a Change is very conceiveable; but it cannot be imagined that what we call Death can be a greater; nor can I believe it will be ſo great a Change, it being highly probable that Seeing, Hearing, and ſome neceſſary Inſtances of Feeling, are common to both our preſent and future State, and a Fund to begin with (together with our intellectual and moral Accompliſhments) when we enter upon that new Condition, wherein I can conceive that other and more exquiſite Senſes may be added to theſe, and not only theſe Senſes, but alſo our Underſtandings, Memory and Activity, may be advanced to a much greater Perfection than they had before. And inaſmuch as our Happineſs muſt imply Society and Intercourſe with each other, and with the external World about us, it cannot be imagined but that we ſhall go off, and be always attended and connected with fine ſenſible Vehicles,* as Means to render us ſenſible to each other, and capable of mutual Communication, and of Intercourſe with the ſenſible

* Vide *Wollaſton, R. N.* Page 197, and *Hierocles*, &c.
& Bp Berkley's Siris § 171.

ſible World around us, wherein the Deity ſo glorioufly diſplays his infinite Perfections.

§ 20. FURTHERMORE, to add another Reſemblance: I ſee here a Multitude of deſpicable Worms, confined to a ſlow Motion, and to a few low grovelling Senſations and Enjoyments, which, after a ſhort Period of ſeeming Death, by a wonderful Transformation, turn into beautiful winged Animals, and waft themſelves at Pleaſure through the Air, and enjoy Pleaſures they were before incapable of. Now may it not be reaſonably thought, that theſe Creatures were deſigned to be Emblems of my own Caſe? I am here, like them, confined to a little Compaſs of Ground, and a few ſlow Motions, feeble Exertions, and low, and comparatively mean Enjoyments.* But if I ſhall have acted my Part well, in Proportion to what Powers and Advantages I now enjoy, may I not reaſonably hope, after my ſeeming Death, to paſs into a new and glorious State, compared with which, my preſent Enjoyments are, in a Manner, contemptible, and my preſent Life little better than a Dream? May I not hope, that when I am freed from this groſs unweildy Body, and from my preſent Limitations and Confinements, and from all my Diſeaſes, Sins and Temptations, to have my Powers greatly enlarged, and to be furniſhed with a pure ætherial Vehicle; and in that Capacity to ſhift the Scene at pleaſure, and traverſe through the vaſt Fields of *Æther*, † and in Company with || other pure Spirits, enjoy Pleaſures inexpreſſible, in the Contem-

* For other Analogies, ſee Biſhop *Butler*.

† *Parte tamen meliore mei ſuper alta perennis*
Aſtra ferar. OVID.

|| Vide *Tull. de Seneɛ̃t.*

templation of GOD, and all His wondrous Works of Nature, Providence and Grace, intirely devoted to the Obedience of His most righteous and reasonable Laws, and unspeakably happy in His Image and Favour.

§ 21. Upon the Whole, therefore, as I cannot conceive how the true End of my Being, especially of that superior Nature, which is the peculiar Character of our Species, can be answered meerly by living this wretched, short and uncertain Life, that is allotted to me here; so I must be persuaded, that I am designed for some other and nobler Condition of Being hereafter, and cannot avoid having *Hopes full of Immortality.* So that the only consistent Notion I can frame of this Life must be this, That as it is the first Stage of my Being, so it is designed only for a State of Childhood, Discipline and *Probation*, in order to another, and a better State, hereafter, which, in the Result, is to be a State of perfect Manhood and *Retribution.* And consequently, that in order to qualify myself for that happy Condition, it must be my greatest Care, and the most important Business of my Life, while I continue here, to acquire, and improve myself in, all those Accomplishments, both of *Knowledge* and *Virtue*, and that both *personal* and *social*, wherein the Perfection and Happiness of my superior rational and immortal Nature consists; which alone I can carry with me into that *future State*; and which alone can enable me to enjoy myself, and my Friends, and, above all, my GOD, who is my supreme and sovereign Good, in whose Favour, with these Accomplishments, I cannot fail of being, in some good Degree, happy even here, and finally secure from all Evil, and in the Enjoyment of a vast,

vaſt, an unſpeakable, and an endleſs Felicity! Thus it appears, that the true and ultimate End of my Being, can be nothing ſhort of this; that I may be as happy as my Condition will admit of here, and eternally and completely happy in the future State of my Exiſtence, in the Enjoyment of GOD, and all that is good, and in the Perfection of Knowledge and Virtue, which alone can render me capable thereof.

PART II.

The *Practical* PART of MORAL PHILOSOPHY.

CHAP. I.

Of the Duties *in general, resulting from the foregoing* Truths.

§ 1. (II.) HAVING thus considered the Nature of my Being, and of that glorious *Cause*, from whom I derive, and on whom I depend, and observed, from the Structure of my Nature, and His Attributes, what I must suppose to have been the great End of that Being and Nature which He hath given me; I proceed now, from the Truths I have found in the *first* or *speculative* Part of this *Essay*, to deduce the *Duties* that result from them, which constitute the *second* or *practical* Part of it.

§ 2. AND, in general, from the Nature and End of my Being, which I have considered, I must conclude, that it is my *Duty*, in Faithfulness to *myself*, *i. e.* to that Nature and those Powers which are given me, as being a reasonable, active and immortal Creature, and in Faithfulness to that

that glorious Being, who is the Author and Preserver of them, to be freely engaged and active myself, in endeavouring to answer His End in the Bestowment of them, which, from the Nature of my Being, I find is to be accomplished by Means of my own Activity (Part I. Chap. I. § 10. And Chap. III. § 7.) And since I am accountable to Him, for all the Powers and Talents He hath bestowed upon me, and must expect He will call me to Account for them, and see what Regard I have had to His End, in the Bestowment of them; it is necessary that I be, above all Things, concerned to act and conduct myself in such a Manner, as to be able to give a good Account of myself to Him. And in order thereunto, I proceed to the

§ 3. (IV.) *FOURTH Enquiry*, and ask myself further, *What I ought to be?* Or, which is the same Thing, *What I ought to do*, in order to answer the End of my Being? Or, what are the necessary Means which do, in the Nature of Things, directly tend to the Accomplishment of it? And for the Resolution of this Enquiry, it will be needful to consider a little more particularly the End itself, which is GOD's End, and, for the same Reason, must be mine; for, from the Nature of the End, we may, in some good Measure, discover what are those Means, whether more immediate or remote, that do naturally tend to the Attainment of it.* To this Purpose therefore, I must reason in the following Manner.

§ 4. THE great End of my Being, is, that my rational and immortal Nature may be completely

* *Quoties quid fugiendum sit, aut quid petendum voles scire, ad summum bonum & propositum totius vitæ respice.* Sen. Ep. 71.

pletely and endlesly happy. The Happineſs of my *rational Nature* conſiſts in that Pleaſure and Satisfaction that naturally attends its being conſcious to itſelf of its Union with its proper Objects. The proper Object of the *Intellect* is *Truth*, and that of the *Will* and *Affections* is *Good* (*Introd.* 5. And Part I. Chap. I. § 5, 6.) ſo that the higheſt Happineſs of our Nature muſt conſiſt in that Pleaſure that attends our *Knowledge of Truth*, and our *chuſing* and *delighting* in *Good*; and conſequently the Purſuit of theſe, muſt, in general, be the great *Duty* of my Life.

§ 5. GOD is *Truth* and *Good* itſelf, and the great Source of all that Truth and Good that is every where to be found in all His Works (Part I. Chap. II. § 6, 7, 8, 10.) Therefore GOD Himſelf, with all the Truth and Good that is contained or implied in Him, and derived from Him, ſo far forth as I can attain to the practical Knowledge of it, muſt neceſſarily be the proper Object of my rational and active Powers, or the Powers of my reaſonable and immortal Nature; and conſequently He muſt be my chief Good, objectively conſidered. And accordingly, in Correſpondence to the Object, my *Duty* and *Happineſs* (which is my chief Good *formally* conſidered) muſt conſiſt in knowing, chuſing, loving, and acquieſcing in Him, and in reſembling or being like Him, as far as ever I am able: In a Word, in the Contemplation and Love of Him, and all that Truth and Good which flows from Him; and in forming the Temper of my Heart, and the Conduct of my Life, conformable thereunto. And this being my true Perfection and Happineſs, muſt moſt certainly be His Will and Law, who wills my Happineſs as

His

His End in giving me my Being, and in all His Diſpenſations towards me. (Part I. Chap III. § 6, 7, 10.)

§ 6. FROM hence it followeth, that my Duty and Happineſs muſt, in general, conſiſt in the Union of my Will with His; in ſincerely chuſing what He chuſeth, and delighting in whatſoever He delights in; in ſubmitting to whatever *Inſtructions* He ſhall think fit to give, or whatever *Laws* He ſhall think fit to enjoin, either by *Nature* or *Revelation*; and in reſigning to the whole Syſtem or *Conſtitution* which He hath eſtabliſhed, both *natural* and *moral*: And conſequently, in patiently bearing whatever He is pleaſed to allot, and in conducting towards every Perſon and Thing, as being what it really is, and what He hath made it, as He Himſelf doth, and in governing myſelf in my whole Temper and Behaviour, by all thoſe Rules which promote the general Weal of the whole Syſtem, as GOD doth Himſelf; always avoiding what is wrong or hurtful, as being contrary thereunto; and doing what is right or beneficial, as being agreeable to it, on all Occaſions as they offer. And all this I muſt do with a hearty Well-meaning, in a deſigned Compliance with His Will, and from a Senſe of Duty and Gratitude to Him, as the great Creator and Governor of the World, and the Father and Friend of Mankind (Part I. Chap. II. § 19.) and ſtedfaſtly perſevere in ſuch a Conduct, in ſpite of all Temptations to the contrary (*Introd.* 6.) This is what is implied in the general Duties of *Sincerity* and *Integrity*.

§ 7. I MUST, therefore, in order hereunto, duly exerciſe my Underſtanding, in acquainting myſelf with the whole Conſtitution of Things,

and

and in making from thence a juſt Eſtimate among the ſeveral Kinds and Degrees of *Good* and *Evil*; and always prefer a *greater* Good before a *leſs*, and a *leſſer* Evil before a *greater*. And, becauſe the *Soul* is by far more excellent than the *Body*; the Intereſt of the *whole Community* much greater than that of any one *Individual*; and *Eternity* of vaſtly more Importance than *Time*; I muſt, therefore, willingly ſuffer *bodily Evils*, to avoid *ſpiritual*; *private*, to prevent *publick*; and *temporal*, in order to ſecure againſt thoſe that are *Eternal*. And I muſt reſign the Goods of the *Body*, or the animal Nature, to thoſe of the *Soul*; *private* Goods, to thoſe of the *Publick*; and the Goods of *Time*, to thoſe of *Eternity*. (*Introd.* 10.)

§ 8. The *Divine Law*, which is immutable Truth, is, in itſelf, the Rule or Standard, conformable to which we are to form our Judgments, and to chuſe and act with regard to theſe ſeveral Goods: But the immediate Rule as to us, can be no other than the inward Senſe of our own Reaſon and *Conſcience* duly informed, which is that Judgment we make of our Tempers and Actions, according to what Senſe or Apprehenſion we have of Right and Wrong, or what we take to be conformable or contrary to that Law. And this Judgment muſt antecedently determine what we ought to do and avoid, and will conſequently give Sentence, whether we have done well or ill. (*Introd.* 15, 22. And Part I. Chap. I. § 6.) Hence ariſeth the Diſtinction of our Actions, into ſuch as are either *materially* or *formally* good or evil. If our Actions are ſuch as are really agreeable to the Rule, and productive of Happineſs, they are ſaid to be *materially* good, even tho' we have no Senſe of Duty, or good

Inten-

Intention in what we do: But in order that an Action be *formally Good*, it is neceſſary, not only that it be conformable to the Rule, but that it be done from a Senſe of Duty, and with an Intention to do what is right and well pleaſing to GOD; *Evil* the contrary. It is therefore a Matter of the higheſt Importance, that I faithfully endeavour to inform my Conſcience, what it is my Duty to do and avoid, as being agreeable or contrary to the divine Law; that in *doubtful* Caſes, I ſuſpend Acting till I have uſed all the Means in my Power, and duly endeavoured to inform myſelf; and that having ſo done, I do religiouſly and ſtedfaſtly endeavour to act up to the Dictates of my own Conſcience thus informed, and this from a Senſe of Duty to that GOD on whom I depend, and to whom I am accountable (Part I. Chap. II. § 19.) If after all my beſt Care, in the Circumſtances in which He has placed me, I have made a Miſtake, I may hope in His Goodneſs, that He will excuſe me, and accept of my Sincerity; but this I can in no wiſe expect, if my Miſtake was occaſioned either by ſupine Negligence, or any criminal Paſſion.

§ 9. AND that my Conſcience may be thoroughly and univerſally informed in all the Branches of my Duty; and in as much as my Happineſs depends on my conducting right in the Whole, as I ſtand variouſly ſituated and related, I muſt deſcend to Particulars, and duly conſider myſelf in all the Relations wherein I ſtand, that I may affect and behave myſelf ſuitably to them, and ſo be happy in each of them. And they may all be reduced to theſe three general Heads, *viz.* To *myſelf*, *my GOD*, and *my Neigh-*

Neighbour; correſpondent to which are the general Duties of *Temperance*, *Piety* and *Benevolence*. Particularly, I. My *firſt* Relation is to *myſelf*, which obligeth me, in Faithfulneſs to myſelf, to behave ſuitably to that rational, active and immortal Nature, which GOD hath given me, that I may be happy in that; and this is called *Human Virtue*,* or Virtue due to that *Human Nature* whereof I conſiſt, and may be expreſſed by the general Term *Temperance*. II. My *ſecond* Relation is to GOD, my Maker, Preſerver and Governor, which obligeth me, in Faithfulneſs to Him, as well as to myſelf, to behave myſelf ſuitably to the Character of ſuch a glorious Being as He is on whom I depend, that I may be happy in Him: And this is *Divine Virtue*, or Virtue due to the *DEITY*, and may be expreſſed by the general Term *Piety*. III. My *third* Relation is to my Fellow Creatures, and eſpecially thoſe of my own Species, of the ſame rational, ſocial and immortal Nature with myſelf, which obligeth me, both in Faithfulneſs to myſelf and others, to behave ſuitably to the ſocial Character, or in ſuch a Manner as is fit, decent and right, towards ſuch a Syſtem of Beings as they are, that I may be happy in them, and they in me; and this is called *Social Virtue*, or Virtue due to *Society*, and may be expreſſed by the general Term *Benevolence*. So that every Branch of Virtue is, in Effect, an Inſtance of *Juſtice* or Righteouſneſs, which implieth, in the general Notion of it, rendering what is due, or treating every Perſon and Thing as being what it really is.

§ 10. THESE *Relations*, and the *Duties* correſpondent to them, are ſaid to be, in the general Nature

* Vide Dr. *Scott*, Part I.

Nature of them, of eternal and immutable Obligation; becauſe if I or other Creatures had never exiſted, or ſhould be no more, and ſo the Fact ſhould ceaſe; yet it is, and always was, and ever will be, impoſſible to conceive of ſuch a Being as I am, and ſo ſituated, to myſelf, my Maker, and my Fellow Creatures, but that theſe Obligations will immutably take hold of me; it being neceſſarily implied in the very Notion of ſuch a Creature in ſuch a Situation, that he ſhould be obliged to ſuch a Conduct (*Introd.* 11.) And as the general Notion of *Sincerity* or *Probity* implieth the Performance of theſe Duties, as well in the inward Temper and Diſpoſition of our Hearts, as in the outward Actions or Behaviour of our Lives, I muſt accordingly conſider it as my firſt Care, to lay a good Foundation within, and to aim at nothing but the Truth and Right of the Caſe upon all Occaſions, in Oppoſition to all Hypocriſy, ſince, in the right Performance of theſe Duties, conſiſts the higheſt Perfection and Happineſs of my rational, ſocial and immortal Nature. (Part. I. Chap. III. § 11. 12.)

C H A P. II.

Of the Duties *which we owe to* ourſelves.

§ 1. (I.) IT is therefore neceſſary, in order to anſwer the End of my Being, *by being what I ought to be*, that I firſt begin at home, and conſider ſeriouſly what the Duties are that I owe to myſelf, which are called *Human Virtues*, and may be comprehended under the general Term, *Tempe-*

Temperance, or a right Government of all my Powers, Appetites and Paſſions, being due to that human, active and immortal Nature, which GOD hath given me, as being neceſſary to its Happineſs within itſelf. And I the rather begin with theſe, as being neceſſary in order to both the other Branches. And,

§ 2. (1.) FROM what hath been ſaid, it is plain, That the *firſt* Duty incumbent upon me, as a reaſonable active Creature, in order to anſwer the End of my Being, is, to cultivate and improve the *Reaſon* and Underſtanding which GOD hath given me, to be the governing Principle and great Law of my Nature (Part I. Chap. III. § 7.) to ſearch and know the *Truth*, and find out wherein my true Happineſs conſiſts, and the Means neceſſary to it, and from thence the Meaſures of *Right* and *Wrong*, and to diſcipline and regulate my Will, Affections, Appetites and Paſſions, according to Reaſon and Truth, that I may freely and readily embrace the one, and reject the other, in order that I may be truly happy. This general Virtue is called *Moral Wiſdom* or *Prudence*, and ſtands in Oppoſition to *Indiſcretion* and *Incogitancy*. And, to deſcend to Particulars;

§ 3. (2.) Becauſe *Pride* conſiſteth in a miſerable Deluſion, in thinking of Things otherwiſe than as being what they really are, and particularly in having too great an Opinion of ourſelves, which is a Temper utterly deſtructive of all Improvement and Proficiency either in Knowledge or Virtue, and odious in the Sight both of GOD and Man; and ſince I am nothing of myſelf, and am intirely dependent on GOD for all that I am, and have, and hope for; and am at the ſame

ſame time conſcious of ſo many Sins and Infirmities, and other humbling Conſiderations, with reſpect both to my Body and Mind, and every Thing about me (Part I. Chap. I. § 14, 15, 16.) It is in the next Place incumbent upon me, to conſider ſeriouſly and *know myſelf*, and *not to think of myſelf more highly than I ought to think, but to think ſoberly*, according to what I really am. And this Virtue is called *Humility*, which is the true Foundation of all others, as it makes us very cautious of our own Conduct, and lays us proſtrate before the DEITY, and diſpoſeth us to treat others with great Temper, Tenderneſs and Affability; and ſtands in Oppoſition to every Degree of *Pride*, *Arrogance*, and *Self-ſufficiency*. And,

§ 4 (3.) As our *Reaſon* and Conſideration is manifeſtly given us to make a juſt Eſtimate of Things, and to preſide over our inferior Powers, and to proportion our ſeveral *Appetites* and *Paſſions*, to the real Nature, and intrinſic Value of their reſpective Objects (Part I. Chap. III. § 7.) ſo as not to *love* or *hate*, *hope* or *fear*, *joy* or *grieve*, be *pleaſed* or *diſpleaſed* at any Thing, beyond the real Importance of it to our Happineſs or Miſery, in the Whole of our Nature and Duration; it muſt therefore be my Duty to keep a due Ballance among them, to keep them within their proper Bounds, and to take Care that they do not exceed or fall ſhort of the real Nature and Meaſure of their ſeveral Objects; and eſpecially ſo as not to ſuffer them to tempt or hurry me on to treſpaſs upon any of the Duties that I owe either to GOD or Man. This is the Office of that Virtue which is called *Moderation* or *Equanimity*, and ſtands in Oppoſition to all *ungoverned Lusts* and *Passions*. More particularly,

§ 5. (4.) BECAUSE *animal Appetites*, and *fleshly Lusts* (I mean the Appetites to Meat and Drink, and other carnal Pleasures, and whatsoever else is of the *concupiscible* Kind) *do war against the Soul*, and an immoderate Indulgence to them doth sensualize and enervate, and, by Consequence, miserably debase and weaken its superior and noble Powers, and alienate them from their proper Objects, and at the same time extremely hurt the Temperature and Health of the Body, and may be very mischievous to others as well as myself, and utterly disqualify me for the Service, Enjoyment and Favour of GOD (Part I. Chap. I. § 15.) it must therefore be my Duty to maintain a perpetual War with them, to curb and restrain them, *to keep them under*, *and bring them into Subjection*, and regulate them by the Ends designed by GOD and Nature, in planting them in us; which is the Office of the Virtues called *Temperance* (strictly so called) or *Sobriety* and *Chastity*, which stand in Opposition to all *Intemperance* and *Debauchery*. And,

§ 6. (5.) WHEREAS the turbulent Passions of *Anger*, *Grief* and *Fear* (*i. e.* Displeasure and Uneasiness at what we already feel or imagine, and anxious Apprehensions of what may seem impending, or whatever else is of the *Irascible* Kind) are apt to warp and byass our Minds, and disable us for a right Judgment and Conduct; to destroy the Peace and Tranquility of our Minds, and create a wretched Tumult within our own Breasts, and frequently prompt us to injurious Words and Actions on the one Hand, or mean Compliances on the other (*Ibid.*) it must there-

therefore be my Duty to keep them alſo, as far as may be, under the due Government of my Reaſon, and not to ſuffer them much to ruffle and diſcompoſe me, much leſs to tyrannize over me, or any ways diſable me for any Duty I owe either to GOD or Man, or tempt me to any Thing injurious to others, or miſchievous to Society: Which is the Office of thoſe Virtues that are called *Meekneſs*, *Patience* and *Fortitude*, which ſtand in Oppoſition to *Wrath*, *Hatred*, *Impatience* and *Puſillanimity*.

§ 7. (6.) FORASMUCH as I am placed by GOD in the Station I am in, whatever it be, and He expects I ſhould faithfully diſcharge the Duties of it, in Proportion to the Powers and Abilities He hath given me; and hath made my own Diligence and Activity in the Uſe of them, the natural Means of my Well-being and Uſefulneſs, excluſive of immoderate Cares and Deſires (Part I. Chap. I. § 10. And Chap. II. § 19, 20.) it muſt therefore be my Duty to reſign to His Diſpoſitions, and to acquieſce in His Allotments, to keep my Station, and reſt ſatisfied with the Condition in which He hath placed me, and contentedly and chearfully diſcharge the Duties of it; and be active and induſtrious in the Uſe of the Powers and Talents He hath furniſhed me with, both for my own Advantage, and the Good of others; for the Benefit of the Publick as well as myſelf; for my comfortable Subſiſtence in this Life, and my everlaſting Happineſs in the Life to come; all which are the Buſineſs of thoſe Virtues which are called *Contentment*, *Frugality* and *Induſtry*, in Oppoſition to *Diſcontent*, *Envy*, *Avarice*, *Ambition* and *Idleneſs*.

§ 8. (7.) AND *lastly:* Inasmuch as I am to continue in my present State but for a short and uncertain Time, and am surrounded with many Troubles and Difficulties, and am placed in a State of *Probation* here, for an eternal State of *Retribution* hereafter; and since that future State of Existence is, consequently, of the vastest Importance to me, and will be more or less happy or miserable, according as I behave myself while I continue here (Part I. Chap. II. § 19. And Chap. III. § 21.) it must therefore be the most important Duty of my Life, while I continue in this present Condition, to be, in a good Measure, disengaged from this World, and from my Body and Time, and to provide in the best Manner I can, for the endless State which is before me; and, in order hereunto, to be daily improving my Soul in Knowledge and Virtue (especially the following Virtues, both *divine* and *social)* and to be disciplining and training up myself in all those Accomplishments and Qualifications, which alone can be of any Use to me when I am called off this present Stage, and which will prepare me to be inconceivably and everlastingly happy in the Life to come. This Duty is called, the *Care of the Soul*, in Opposition to the excessive *Love of the World*, and *the Body*. And thus much for the *Duties* we owe to *ourselves*.

CHAP.

CHAP. III.

Of the Duties *we owe to* GOD.

§ 1. (II.) I PROCEED now, in the *ſecond* Place, to the Conſideration of the Relation we ſtand in to Almighty GOD. In Purſuance of which, it is neceſſary that I ſeriouſly conſider what is due to the Character of ſuch a glorious Being, as reſulting from that Relation I ſtand in to Him, in order that I may be happy in Him; or what thoſe Duties are which I owe to that All-wiſe, Almighty and moſt juſt and benevolent Being, from whom I derive, and on whom I depend; which are called the *Divine Virtues*, and are comprehended under the general Name *Piety*; without the faithful Performance of which, I ſhall rob Him of His juſt Due, in not conducting towards Him, as being what He is, and at the ſame time rob myſelf of the greateſt Happineſs, as He is my chief Good. And,

§ 2. (1.) INASMUCH as GOD is a Being of all poſſible Perfection and Excellency, the great Creator, Preſerver and Governor of the World, on whom I do intirely depend for my Being, and all my Enjoyments here, and all my Hopes to all Eternity, and to whom I am accountable for all that I think, ſpeak and do (Part I. Chap. II. § 19.) it is therefore my indiſpenſible Duty in general, to own and *acknowledge* Him, and to live under a deep, ſerious and habitual Senſe of Him as ſuch, and to *believe* in Him, and *faithfully* endeavour to *obey* and pleaſe Him in all my

Behaviour. This Duty is called the *Knowledge* or *Acknowledgment* of GOD, and *Faith* or *Faithfulness* to Him; and stands in Opposition to the *Ignorance* of Him, and *Atheism* and *Unbelief*, and to a *Neglect* of Him, and *Disregard* to His Authority and Government. And,

§ 3. (2.) BECAUSE GOD is a Being of infinite Perfection and Excellency, and therefore infinitely amiable in Himself, and is also the great Parent Mind, and universal Father of Spirits, and the Source of all Beauty, Order and Happiness, and is accordingly, as a tender Parent, unspeakably kind and benevolent to me, and to all the World, and continually doing Good, and providing every Thing needful for my Subsistence and Well being; and by what He is, and has done for me hitherto, hath given me all the Reason imaginable to believe, that if I faithfully endeavour to resemble and please Him, He will not fail to make me for ever as happy as my Capacity will admit of (*Ibid.* And Chap. III. § 16, 17, 20.) it must therefore be my Duty to *love* and delight in Him, as my chief Good, *gratefully* to acknowledge His Bounty and Beneficence, to *prefer* Him and His Service before all Things, and to be wholly *devoted* to Him, both in the sincere Intentions of my Heart, and the whole Conduct of my Life. This Duty is called *Love* and *Gratitude* to GOD, in Opposition to all *Ingratitude* and *Hatred* or *Aversion* to Him and His Service. And,

§ 4. (3.) SINCE GOD is infinitely sufficient to all the Purposes of my Happiness; has infinite Wisdom to direct Him, Power to enable Him, and Goodness to incline Him to assist me, in the Discharge of all my Duties, to support me under

under all Difficulties, to keep me from whatſoever may hinder or interrupt my Well-being, and to ſecure to me every Thing that is requiſite to my Happineſs (*Ibid.*) it muſt therefore be my Duty to *confide* in Him intirely, in the Way of *Well-doing*, with a ſecure *Acquieſcence* in His All wiſe and All-powerful Goodneſs, which, in one Word, is His *All-ſufficiency*. This Duty is called *Truſt*, or *Confidence* in GOD, in Oppoſition to all *Diſtruſt* and *Diffidence*. And,

§ 5. (4.) FORASMUCH as GOD is thus infinitely benevolent, wiſe and powerful, and cannot but know what is beſt for me, infinitely better than I do myſelf, and cannot be miſled or controuled in any Diſpoſitions He is pleaſed to make concerning me, and will not fail to bring Good out of Evil, and to make Evil ſubſervient to Good, and to bring about the beſt Ends by the fitteſt Means; nor can He fail to conſult the beſt Good in the Whole, in all His Commands and Diſpenſations, in every Thing He requireth me to do or ſuffer (*Ibid.* And Chap. II. § 24, 25.) it muſt therefore be my Duty to be entirely *reſigned* to Him, to *ſubmit* to His Orders and Allotments, and to have my Will always, as far as poſſible, united with His. This is the Duty of *Submiſſion* and *Reſignation* to GOD, in Oppoſition to all *Murmuring*, *Untowardneſs* and *Rebellion*. And,

§ 6. (5.) BECAUSE GOD is the incomprehenſibly great and tremendous moral Governor of the World; as there is nothing that I may not hope for from His Goodneſs, that is really ſubſervient to my beſt Good, if I faithfully endeavour to obey and pleaſe Him; ſo, on the other Hand, from His Diſpleaſure and Juſtice, I can-

 not

not but expect the severest Punishments, if I live in Opposition to His Will, who is constantly present with me, and sees all the Tempers of my Heart, and Actions of my Life, and will, in a little Time, call me to Account for them (Part I. Chap. II. § 19.) it must therefore be my Duty always to stand in *Awe* of Him, and to think and speak of Him in the most *reverend* Manner; to *set Him ever before me*, as a Witness and Spectator of all my Behaviour, and to be above all Things concerned not to displease Him, and solicitously careful, to approve myself to Him in all that I do. This Duty is called *Reverence*, or the *Fear* of GOD, in Opposition to all *Irreverence* and *Disregard* towards Him. And,

§ 7. (6.) SINCE GOD is Himself infinitely Holy, True, Just and Good, and consequently the great Pattern and Standard of all moral Perfection, and since it is evident, from the intelligent, free, active Nature, that He hath given me, that I am capable of some good Degree of Resemblance or Likeness to Him, and since by how much the more I resemble Him, by so much the more perfect and happy I shall certainly be (Part I. Chap. II. § 5.) I must therefore think it my Duty to be as *like* Him as ever I can, in all my Tempers and Deportment; *Holy* as He is *Holy*, *Righteous* as He is *Righteous*, *True* and *Faithful*, *Kind* and *Merciful* as He is. This Duty is called the *Imitation* of GOD, in Opposition to *Unholiness*, or being *unlike* to Him.

§ 8. (7.) AND *lastly*, since GOD is that Being from whom we receive all that we enjoy, and on whom we depend for all that we want both for Time and Eternity (Part I. Chap. II. § 6. and Chap. III. § 16.) and since it is fit and right

right in itſelf that we own him to be what he is, and of great Advantage to us that we live under a deep and habitual Senſe of this our Dependence upon him, and our Obligations to him; and that Gratitude requireth our juſt Acknowledgments; it muſt therefore be our bounden Duty, to all theſe good Purpoſes, and for the improving in us every Kind of Virtue, that we do, every Day that we live, moſt gratefully *praiſe* him for every Thing we receive, and *pray* to him for all that we want; and we live a moſt unnatural and brutiſh Life, if we neglect ſo to do. And becauſe we cannot do this with any Meaning, without that Love, Truſt, Reſignation, Reverence and Imitation, which I have demonſtrated to be our Duties towards him; therefore theſe Tempers and Diſpoſitions muſt ever be ſuppoſed to attend all our Prayers and Praiſes, which are comprehended under the general Name of *Devotion*, or the *Worſhip* of GOD, in Oppoſition to all *Profaneneſs*, *Irreligion*, *Superſtition* and *Idolatry*.

§ 9. AND inaſmuch as Mankind do thus depend upon GOD, and receive innumerable Favours from Him, not only in their ſingle, but alſo in their ſocial Capacity; and as there is a peculiar Fitneſs in it, as we are all Children of the ſame common Parent, the great *Father of Spirits*, that we ſhould, not only ſeverally, but jointly, as Brethren, pay our common Homage, and teſtify our grateful Senſe of our common Dependence and Obligations; and as our joint Performance of this Duty does open Honour to Him in the World, and hath, at the ſame time, a natural Tendency, the more ardently to affect our Hearts with Devotion to Him, as well as to unite us the more ſtrongly in mutual Bene-

Benevolence one towards another: It is therefore *fit, right, and our bounden Duty*, to worſhip GOD, not only ſeverally, but alſo jointly, in our *Families*, and in publick *Communities*, upon ſuch ſtated Seaſons, and in ſuch Forms, Geſtures and other Circumſtances, as are generally agreed upon to be moſt expreſſive of Reverence, Duty and Devotion to him. This is the great Duty of *publick Worſhip*; to the honourable Support of which, we ought, therefore, both for GOD's Sake and our own, jointly and liberally to contribute. And thus much for our Duty towards GOD.

CHAP. IV.

Of the Duties which we owe to our Fellow Creatures, *or to thoſe of our own* Species *and* Society *in general, and to our* Relatives *in particular.*

§ 1. (III.) I Proceed now, in the *third* Place, to the Conſideration of the Relation we ſtand in one to another: In Purſuance of which, it is neceſſary that I ſeriouſly conſider what is due to the ſocial Character as reſulting from that Relation; or what thoſe Duties are which I owe to my Fellow Creatures, eſpecially thoſe of my own Species, which are called *Social Virtues*; and are comprehended under the general Term, *Benevolence*, of which they are ſo many Branches; and they conſiſt in general, in treating or behaving towards them as being what they and I are, that

I may be happy in them, and they in me. And as to theſe,

§ 2. (1.) SINCE, as I have above obſerved, being furniſhed with Reaſon and Speech, and ſocial Affections, we are evidently made for Society (Part I. Chap. I. §. 13.) and ſince we are placed, by the Condition of our Nature, not only in a State of Dependence on Almighty GOD, our common Heavenly Parent, but alſo in a State of mutual Dependence on each other for our Well-being and Happineſs (for that in many Caſes we cannot well ſubſiſt without each others Help, and by the good or ill Uſe of our Powers, we are capable of being either very uſeful, or very miſchievous to each other) and ſince, by the Powers of Reflection and Reaſoning, we are enabled to place ourſelves in each other's Stead, and to make a Judgment from what we feel in ourſelves, how we ſhould wiſh to be uſed by others, and to diſcover what is beſt in the Whole, for our common Safety and mutual Advantage (*Introd.* 17.) it is from theſe Conſiderations manifeſt, that, in general, it muſt be our Duty to conſider ourſelves as ſuch, and ſo ſituated and related, as in Fact we are, and to cultivate a hearty good Will one towards another as Brethren; to do nothing hurtful, and all that is beneficial to each other, as far as we may or can, and to enter into Combinations and Compacts for promoting our common Intereſt and Safety; to reſign every one his own private Advantage to that of the Community, in which his own is beſt ſecured, and to make the common Good the Standard by which to judge of his own Duty and Intereſt, and be inflexibly governed by it. Such, in general, is the Diſpoſition of *Benevolence*, which, taking

taking its Riſe in the firſt Connections of the Individuals, ſpreads thro' the whole ſocial Syſtem, and iſſues in, and ſtrongly prompts to *publick Virtue*, and the *Love* of our *Country*, and our *Species*, in Oppoſition to every Thing that implies *Malevolence*, *Selfiſhneſs* and *private Spiritedneſs*. But to be particular in its ſeveral Branches riſing from the loweſt to the higheſt:

§ 3. (2.) INASMUCH as I have ſeveral Things which I call *my own*, to which I have a *Right*, being poſſeſſed of them either by the free Gift of God, or by my own Activity and Induſtry, with his Bleſſing, and find they are greatly uſeful to my Comfort and Well-being, and feel a great Pleaſure in the unmoleſted Enjoyment of them, and Trouble in being deprived of them: And when I am moleſted or deprived by any One, without having juſtly forfeited them by my own Miſconduct, I feel a ſtrong Senſe of Injury, and muſt therefore by Reflection conclude, that every other Perſon hath the ſame Senſe of Injury in the like Caſe as I have; it muſt therefore be my Duty, and the firſt Dictate of *Benevolence*, not to do Injury to others in any Reſpect, whether it relates to their Souls, Bodies, Names or Eſtates, *&c.* and the rather, as I would wiſh to ſuffer no Injury from them in any of theſe Reſpects. (Part I. Chap. I. § 7.) This Diſpoſition is called *Innocence* and *Inoffenſiveneſs*, in Oppoſition to *Injuriouſneſs* and *Miſchievouſneſs*.

§ 4. (3.) PARTICULARLY; ſince I know that I cannot endure to be hurt in my Perſon, either in Soul or Body; to be robbed of my Liberty, Eſtate, Wife or Children; to be belied or miſrepreſented in my Name or Reputation, and to be deceived and impoſed upon, or any wiſe oppreſ-

ſed

ſed in my Dealings, *&c.* as I muſt conclude it to be wrong to treat others ill in any of theſe, or the like Inſtances; ſo, on the other Hand, for the ſame Reaſon that I think it right, that, in Subordination to the publick Senſe and Intereſt (*i. e.* ſuppoſing no Forfeiture) every One ſhould allow me the quiet and peaceable Enjoyment of my own, my Innocence, Life, Limbs, Liberty, Eſtate, Wife, Children, *&c.* and ſpeak nothing but the Truth to me, and of me, and deal equitaby, fairly and faithfully with me, and in every Thing treat me as being what I am and have, (*Ibid.*) I muſt think it right, and my Duty accordingly, from the ſame Principle, to treat others with Equity in all theſe Reſpects, as I would wiſh to be treated by them in the like Circumſtances. And this Duty is called *Juſtice*, in the ſtrict Senſe of it, which comprehends *Examplarineſs*, *Equity*, *Truth* and *Faithfulneſs*, in Oppoſition to all Inſtances of *Injuſtice*; ſuch as, *tempting* to Sin, *Murther*, *Maiming*, *Adultery*, *Fornication*, *Stealth*, *Robbery*, *Oppreſſion*, *Lying*, *Defamation*, *Unfaithfulneſs* to Engagements, *Cheating*, and all *Deceitfulneſs*.

§ 5. (4.) FOR the like Reaſons; ſince I feel a great Delight in being well reſpected, duly eſteem'd, well ſpoken of, and kindly treated by others (Part I. Chap. I. § 13.) I muſt think it my Duty, from the ſame benevolent Principle, to treat others with all ſuch Diſpoſitions, Acts and Inſtances of Kindneſs and good Uſage, as I ſhould, in my Turn, reaſonably expect, and take Pleaſure in receiving; to be ready to all good Offices in my Power to others, whether Neighbours or Strangers, whether to their Souls or Bodies; to ſay the beſt of them,
and

and put the kindest and most favourable Construction I can upon what they say or do; and to conduct towards them with Humanity, Candour, Affability and Courtesy. And as I find a great Solace under Pain and Distress in the Pity and Assistance of others; so I must think it my Duty to have the like Sentiments of Compassion and Tenderness towards them in the like Circumstances, whether of Mind, Body or Estate, and should think I acted unnaturally, if I did not contribute all I could, consistent with other Obligations, to their Comfort and Relief. Thus by reflecting and conceiving ourselves in each other's Circumstances (Part I. Chap. I. § 5.) our Love to ourselves becomes the Foundation of our Love to others, and causeth us to take Pleasure in their Enjoyments, and in communicating Pleasure to them; to delight in good Offices, and in speaking kindly to them, and of them; and to sympathize with them in their Calamities, and be ready to relieve them. All which are implied in the general Duty of *Charity*, which therefore comprehends *Candour*, *Affability*, *Hospitality*, *Mercy*, *Tenderness* and *Beneficence*, in Opposition to all Instances of *Uncharitableness*, such as *Censoriousness*, *Moroseness*, *Envy*, *Ill-nature*, *Cruelty* and *Hardheartedness*.

§ 6. (5.) INASMUCH as it is manifest, from what was observed above, under the first general Head of the Duty we owe to Society, that it is incumbent upon us to do all we can to promote the Weal of our Fellow-Creatures, and to have a principal Zeal for the general Good, on which our own Welfare does very much depend (Part I. Chap. I. § 13. And Part II. Chap. I. § 6.) and since there may be several Things in our Power,

Power, above and beyond what meer Justice and Humanity require, wherein we may be useful to others, and to the Publick; I must think it my Duty, from the same Principle, to be of a free and generous Spirit as far as I am able; to be forward and ready to every good Work, and to delight in doing Good, as GOD himself does, whereinsoever I may be useful in promoting his Honour, and the Good of Mankind; and this from a Sense of Gratitude to him for all I enjoy. This Virtue is called *Liberality*, *Generosity* and *Magnificence*, in Opposition to *Covetousness* and *Niggardliness*, or a *grudging*, *narrow* and *contracted Spirit*. And for any Benefits received either of GOD or Man, *Gratitude* is due to the Benefactor, in Opposition to a stupid *ungrateful Spirit*, which is extremely base and odious.

§ 7. (6.) SINCE the Peace and Quietness of Society, which are indispensably necessary to its Happiness, depend not only on our avoiding every Thing that is injurious, and doing all that is just, kind and generous, but also upon every One's being contented in his own Station, and faithfully endeavouring to discharge the Duties of it, without intermeddling in Affairs that do not belong to his Province; and upon every One's being of a Peace-making and forgiving Spirit, (Part II. Chap. II. § 6.) I must therefore think it my Duty to keep within my own Sphere, and mind my own Business, and do the Duty that belongs to my own Station; and if I have done any Wrong, to repair the Injury, and make Restitution, and ask Forgiveness, as well as to be of a forgiving Spirit towards others, as I would hope GOD to be so towards me; and in a Word, to do all that is in my Power for promoting and preserving

ſerving Friendſhip, good Neighbourhood, and the Publick Tranquility. Theſe Duties are called *Quietneſs*, *Peaceableneſs*, *Friendlineſs*, and *Forgiveneſs*, in Oppoſition to *Ambition*, *Contention*, *Unfriendlineſs*, and *Irreconcileableneſs*.

§ 8. (7.) AND *laſtly*, ſince, according to the preſent Condition of our Nature, it cannot be but various Relations and Connections muſt obtain, as being neceſſary for the Subſiſtence and Well-being of our Species, both in Mind, Body and Eſtate; ſuch as Huſband and Wife, Parents and Children, Maſters and Servants, Magiſtrates and Subjects, Teachers and Learners, *&c.* (Part I. Chap. I. § 13.) it muſt be my Duty, whichſoever of theſe Conditions I am placed in, to behave myſelf ſuitably to it. If I am a *Huſband* or *Wife*, I muſt be tenderly loving, faithful and helpful: If I am a *Parent*, I muſt be tender of my helpleſs Off-ſpring, and do all I can to inſtruct and form both their Minds and Manners to the beſt Advantage, and provide for them in the beſt Manner I am able, conſiſtent with every other Duty: And if I am a *Child*, I muſt be grateful, and tenderly helpful, dutiful and obedient to my Parents, from whom I derived, and on whom I do or have depended, when unable to help myſelf; and have a peculiar Tenderneſs and Friendſhip for my Brethren and Siſters, and other Relatives: If I am a *Maſter*, I muſt be juſt and kind to my Servant; and if I am a *Servant*, I muſt be dutiful, obedient and faithful to my Maſter: If I am a *Magiſtrate*, I muſt be zealous for the publick Good, and upright, faithful and impartial in my Adminiſtration: And if I am *Subject*, I muſt be ſubmiſſive and orderly, in Obedience to Law and Authority: If I am a *Teacher*,

Teacher, I muſt be ready and faithful to guide and inſtruct: And if I am a *Learner*, I muſt be willing to be guided, and ready to follow the Inſtructions that are given me, and to reward the Labours of ſuch as have the Care of me. In a Word, if I am in any *ſuperior* Station of Life, I muſt be treatable and condeſcending; and if in an *inferior* Condition, I muſt be modeſt, reſpectful and decent in all my Deportment; and whatſoever Situation of Life it is, wherein I am placed, I muſt take Care to act up to my Character, whatever it be; both in thoſe leſſer Societies founded in *Nature*, which are called *Families*, and thoſe larger Societies founded in *Compact*, whether tacit or explicit, called *Civil Governments*; to which all *Honour*, *Submiſſion* and *Obedience*, is due in all Things lawful and honeſt, in Oppoſition to all Inſtances of *Turbulence*, *Faction* and *Rebellion*. All which relative Duties, in Conjunction with the reſt, are indiſpenſibly neceſſary to the moral Order, and the publick Peace and Happineſs of Mankind, and terminate in that nobleſt of all ſocial Paſſions, the *Love of our Country*, joined with an ardent Zeal for every Thing that concerns its Weal. And thus much for our Duties towards Society.

CHAP. V.

Of the Subordinate Duties, *or* Means *for the more ready and faithful Diſcharge of the Duties above explained.*

§ 1. HAVING thus deduced, from the great Principles of Truth above demonſtrated, the principal Branches of moral Duty founded on them, both towards GOD, *ourselves*, and our *Neighbours*; I proceed now to enumerate the chief of those *subordinate Duties*, which are to be performed as Means of *Culture*, for begetting, improving and perfecting in us those *moral Virtues*. And this will be done in answer to the two last of those great Enquiries (*Introd.* 27.) *viz.* V. *Whether I am what I ought to be?* And if not, VI. *What I ought to do, as a Means in order to be and do what I ought, and so in order finally to answer the End of my Being?*

§ 2. THE *first* of those two last Enquiries will put us upon the great Duty of *Self-examination*, which is a Duty of very great Importance to us; for if we do not examine and truly *know ourselves*, and what is our real State, how shall we be able to rectify what is amiss, that we may be in a Condition to give a good Account of ourselves at last? And as *Seneca* says, *Illi mors gravis incubat,---qui nimis notus omnibus,---ignotus moritur sibi.* He dies a grievous Death indeed,---who too much known to others, dies---a Stranger to himself!

§ 3. (1.) LET this then be the *first* Rule in order to answer the Demands of these last Questions, and the first Means in order to become what I ought to be, *viz.* To inure myself to a Habit of *serious Consideration*; to suspend Acting, till I have well weighed the Importance of Things (Part I. Chap. I. § 5.) that I may be under Advantage to make a wise Choice; and, according to *Pythagoras*'s Advice to his Disciples *, to enter frequently into my own Heart, and take a daily and exact Survey of my Life and Conduct; to deal faithfully with myself, and to endeavour to think of my Temper and Behaviour, as being what

* *Carm. Aur.* Vide *Hierocles.*

what it really is, *without Partiality, and without Hypocrisy.*

§ 4. (2.) AND as the Knowledge of myself is of so great Importance, let it be the next Rule, that I entertain and cultivate within myself a due Sense of the *Dignity* of my reasonable, active and immortal Nature, as exhibiting a small Image of the Divinity (Part I. Chap. I. § 6, 7, 8. And Chap. II. § 5.) and have a great *Reverence* for it as such: This would make me always careful to do nothing unworthy, indecent or misbecoming it; on the contrary, I should be concerned, on all Occasions, to act the decent Part in Life, or what duly becomes it in all its Relations. Let me especially have a great Reverence for the Sense of my own Conscience, as being the Divine Light irradiating me within, and the Voice of the Deity Himself, that I may take the utmost Care, not to live in any Course whatsoever for which my own Reason and Conscience shall reproach me; for as One's Conscience is properly One's Self, it is the greatest Madness in the World, for a Man to live at a perpetual Variance with himself, and the first Point of Wisdom, always to keep Friends with himself.

§ 5. (3.) SINCE I depend wholly on GOD, and He is ever present with me, a constant Spectator of all my Behaviour, in the inward Temper and Thoughts of my Heart, as well as in all the outward Actions of my Life, and since I must expect to give an Account of myself to Him (Part I. Chap. II. § 9. and 19.) it must be my next Rule, by the frequent Practice of Meditation and Devotion, to possess myself habitually of a most great and *reverend Sense* of His *universal Presence*, All-sufficiency and Purity, as well as a most abasing Sense of my own Dependence, Guilt and Impotence, that I may be awfully careful to do nothing unworthy of His Presence and Inspection, and the Relation I stand in to Him, and seriously endeavour, in a humble Dependence upon His gracious Assistance, so to guard and discipline my Thoughts and Affections, as well as my Words and Actions, that they may not be displeasing to His All-seeing Eye, but may obtain His Favour and Approbation, in whose moral Character is contained all that is perfectly right and amiable in itself, and on whose Approbation and Friendship my Happiness all depends.

§ 6. (4.) IT will also be of very good Use to promote in me every Sort of Virtue, and especially those of the social Kind, to entertain a *great Sense* and *Value* of the *Opinion* and *Estimation* of *Mankind*, who, even the most corrupt of them, and much more the best (whose Esteem is highly to be valued) cannot but entertain a high Opinion of Virtue, and a Reverence and Esteem for the virtuous Character, as well as a Contempt of the Vicious (Part I. Chap. I. § 11.) so that if I have any Desire of either doing any Good to them, or enjoying any Good from them, it must deeply concern me to endeavour to recommend myself to their good Opinion, and this can no otherwise be done, than by always acting the sober, honest, faithful, generous and benevolent Part, in all my Intercourse with them, which cannot fail of engaging an Interest in their Good-will, Esteem and Confidence, and must therefore be the wisest Course I can take to answer all my most important Purposes, with Regard to my comfortable Subsistence in this present Life, as well as to qualify me for a better.

§ 7. (5.) If upon a due Survey of my Temper and Behaviour, I find I have acted an unreasonable and vicious Part, as my own Conscience will not fail to reproach me for it, so I cannot avoid feeling a great Deal of Uneasiness and Remorse upon reflecting on my Misconduct (Part I. Chap. I. § 6. And Chap. III. § 11.) Now whenever I feel any Remorse or Misgivings, I should do wisely to be so far from stifling, that I should rather indulge those Sentiments, and let them have their Course, and improve them into a truly contrite Grief. And if I am sorry for what is amiss in my Conduct, as I ought to be, I shall utterly hate and abhor every Vice, as being contrary to GOD, and all that is right and reasonable, and never be easy till I reform and return to my Duty, and be governed by my Reason and Conscience, and a Sense of Duty to GOD, and every wise and good Consideration, for the Time to come. And herein consists the Nature of true *Repentance* and *Reformation*. And,

§ 8. (6.) If I truly repent of my past Misconduct, I shall be very *watchful* against all those *Temptations* that I find myself exposed to, either from my own Lusts and Passions within, or from the Solicitations of a corrupt and degenerate World without me (Part I. Chap. I. § 15.) As I must consider Virtue to be my greatest Interest, being my true Perfection and Happiness, I shall therefore avoid all ill Places and *bad Company*, where I am most liable to Danger, and consider every Person and Thing as an Enemy that hath a Tendency to rob me of my Innocence, and mislead me from a stedfast Course of virtuous Behaviour; and, by Consequence, I shall account those my best Friends that most promote Virtue by their good Advice, Example, *&c.* and therefore ſhall be ambitious of keeping the *beſt Company*, and following the beſt Examples.

§ 9. (7.) I SHALL carefully obſerve what is my *ruling Paſſion*, and endeavour to make an Advantage of it to promote the Intereſt of Virtue, and againſt all the Tendencies of Vice, and be more eſpecially upon my Guard againſt thoſe particular *Failings*, that I find my own *Conſtitution* is peculiarly incident to, whether of the concupiſcible or iraſcible Kind; whether thoſe of Self-conceit, Luſt, Covetouſneſs, Intemperance, *&c.* on the one Hand, or thoſe of Reſentment, Anger, Impatience, Envy, Revenge, *&c.* on the other; there being, perhaps, ſcarce a Perſon to be found, but hath ſome particular Tendency towards ſome one Vice more than another, founded in the very Frame of his Nature, which adminiſters Matter and Occaſion for particular Humiliation and continual Diſcipline. (Part I. Chap. I. § 15.)

§ 10. (8.) IF I find I have any ſuch particular Tendency, and have contracted any vicious Habit by my Indulgence to it, I muſt inure myſelf to *Self-denial* and *Mortification*, till I have got the Aſcendant of it: I muſt conſider Slavery as a moſt wretched and abject Condition, and therefore never content myſelf, till I have gained and maintain the Maſtery of myſelf, ſo as to be at Liberty readily to follow the Dictates of my Reaſon and Conſcience, and act up to the Dignity of my rational active Nature, and the ſeveral Connections founded in my Relation to GOD and my Fellow Creatures, and ſo become *what I ought to be.* (Part I. Chap. III. § 11.)

§ 11. (9.) IN order that I may *diſcipline* myſelf to a Readineſs in denying myſelf in Things unlaw-

unlawful, and the more effectually tame and subdue my untoward Lusts and Passions, and keep them under a due Regimen; it may be very fit and useful that I frequently practise Self-denial in Things lawful and indifferent; for if I always accustom myself to go to the utmost Bounds of my lawful Liberty, it is a Million to One but I shall be frequently trespassing upon them; for which Reason I should do well, by frequent *Fasting*, to deny myself such Measures or Kinds of Food and Drink, *&c.* as might otherwise be lawfully indulged; and particularly such as have a peculiar Tendency to inflame my Lusts and Passions (Part II. Chap. II. § 4.)

§ 12. (10.) I MUST, from a Sense both of the Glory and Dignity of Virtue, and my Duty to Almighty GOD, *resolutely* go into every virtuous Practice, however so much against the Grain, in which I shall act the truly heroic and manly Part; nor must I content myself in any certain Pitch of Virtue to which I imagine myself to have attained, but must *press forward*, and *persevere* in a continual Struggle, and perpetual Warfare, throughout my whole Life, and be daily endeavouring to make all possible Proficiency in Virtue, till I gain the utmost Facility and Readiness in every virtuous Practice that the Frailty of my Nature will admit of (Part I. Chap. III. § 21.)

§ 13. (11.) IN order to this, I should do well to consider seriously the vast Importance of that inestimable Talent, *Time*, of which I must expect to give an Account to the Author and Preserver of my Being, as well as of all my other Talents. Let therefore an habitual Sense of the Shortness, at the utmost, and of the extreme Uncertainty of my Life, be ever present and uppermost in my Thoughts, that I may husband every Moment to the best Advantage for the doing what good I can, and acquiring of true Wisdom and Virtue, which are Treasures of the most inestimable Value, as being those only which can make me truly useful and happy here, and which alone I can carry with me into the future State of my Existence, and which will make me for ever and compleatly happy, when Time shall be no more (Part I. Chap. III. § 21.)

§ 14. (12.) And, *lastly*, in order to my being the more effectually engaged to the faithful Discharge of my Duty, in conforming to all the Laws of Virtue, I must endeavour to keep up in my Mind an habitual Sense of their most weighty *Sanctions*, *viz.* The Happiness or Misery unavoidably attending my Obedience or Disobedience, both in this and the future State. In this present Life there is the truest Enjoyment of all reasonable Pleasures, without that Remorse and Terror which attends those that are unreasonable and vicious; Health of Body, and Peace of Mind; the Love, Esteem and Confidence of Men, and the Approbation, Favour and Blessing of GOD; true Joy and Satisfaction in Prosperity, and solid Comfort and Calmness in Adversity; the most reasonable Prospect of Success in our Affairs here, and a most comfortable Prospect of Happiness hereafter; so that if there was to be no Life after this, a Course of Virtue would be infinitely preferable to that of Vice, which is unavoidably attended with endless Mischiefs and Perplexities: The Wicked are like the *troubled Sea*, and seldom *live out Half their Days*; whereas, the Ways of Wisdom and Virtue *are Ways*

of

of Pleaſantneſs, and all her Paths are Peace; Length of Days is in her Right-hand, and in her Left-hand Riches and Honour. Sup. 6, and Part I. Chap. III. § 11.

§ 15. BUT then if we look forward to the Life to come, there opens a moſt glorious Proſpect for eternal Ages. As on the one Hand there are moſt tremendous Puniſhments attending our Diſobedience, there being unavoidable Pain and exquiſite Miſery neceſſarily connected with every Vice, ariſing from the Remorſe and Reproaches of our own Minds, and the fearful Apprehenſions and diſmal Effects of the divine Diſpleaſure: So, on the other Hand, there are as certain and moſt glorious Rewards attending a Courſe of Obedience, there being unſpeakable Pleaſure and exquiſite Happineſs neceſſarily connected with the Practice of every Virtue, ariſing both from the natural Fruits and Effects thereof, and from the Approbation and Applauſes of our own Minds; from all the Delights of a happy Society, and from the Favour and Friendſhip of Almighty GOD, to the endleſs Ages of Eternity (Part I. Chap. III. § 11. and II. 19.)

§ 16. IF I diligently attend to theſe Things, and live in the conſtant Practice of them, together with the daily Offices of true Devotion, having thereby a frequent Intercourſe with the great *Father of Spirits*, and Pattern of all Perfection, which vaſtly tends to the Proficiency of Virtue, I ſhall, at length, be ſo inured to the Love and Practice of every Virtue, humane, divine and ſocial, in the Perfection of which conſiſts the higheſt Happineſs of my reaſonable and immortal Nature, that I ſhall at length be prepared to quit this preſent Stage, and to give a good

good Account of myſelf to GOD, being in ſome good Meaſure qualified for that perfect State of Virtue and conſummate Happineſs, which is to be expected in the future State of my Exiſtence; according to that excellent Saying of the wiſe King; *The Path of the Juſt is like the ſhining Light, which ſhineth more and more unto the perfect Day.*

CHAP. VI.

Of the Connection between the Law *or* Religion *of* Nature *and* Chriſtianity.

§ 1. HAVING thus given a ſhort Sketch of the firſt great Principles of *Moral Philoſophy*, or what is called the *Religion* or Law of *Nature*, as being founded in the Nature of GOD and Man, and the Relation between Him and us, and our Relation one to another, in Conformity to which conſiſteth the higheſt Perfection and Happineſs of human Nature, and may therefore be called the *Religion* of the *End**, and alſo the Chief of thoſe ſubordinate Duties ſubſervient thereunto, which may be called the *Religion* of *the Means*: I ſhall now conclude, by giving a very ſhort Summary of *revealed Religion*, and ſhew the Connection between them and CHRISTIANITY, or the Religion of the *Mediator*, which is to be conſidered as the great infallible Means of our Inſtruction and Reformation, for begetting, improving and perfecting in us all the Virtues of an honeſt Heart, and a good

* Dr. *Scott*, P. I.

good Life, and for aſcertaining to us the Favour of GOD, and a bleſſed Immortality; to which it is ſo admirably ſubſervient, that it ſhould ſeem the greateſt Inconſiſtency imaginable for a Man to be a real Friend to what is called Natural Religion or Morality, and at the ſame time not to adhere firmly to the Chriſtian Syſtem.

§ 2. FOR altho' theſe great Truths and Duties appear thus evident and demonſtrable, in the Nature of Things, to any ſerious, thinking and conſiderate Perſon, who hath had Means of Information, and Leiſure to give a proper Attention to them; and many wiſe Men in the Heathen World (doubtleſs much aſſiſted in theſe Enquiries, by Inſtructions handed down to them by Tradition, from the firſt Parents and intermediate Anceſtors of Mankind) have made very great Proficiency in theſe Speculations; yet it muſt be allowed, that ſo many are the Cares and Buſineſſes, and the Pleaſures and Amuſements of this Life, which do unavoidably engage the Attention of the general Rate and Bulk of Mankind, that it cannot be expected they ſhould ever attain to the diſtinct practical Knowledge of them, in their preſent Condition, without Inſtruction from above. So that an expreſs Revelation is highly expedient, and indeed extremely neceſſary, as a Means in order to render Men in any tolerable Meaſure capable of anſwering the End of their Being; eſpecially if it be conſidered, that no Philoſopher or Teacher, without a ſufficiently atteſted Commiſſion from GOD, even if he could diſcover all theſe *Laws of Nature*, could have Authority to enjoin them, as being what indeed they are, the *Laws of GOD*, without which they would make but a ſmall Impreſſion on them;

and

and that this would be the most direct and compendious Method of answering this Purpose *.

§ 3. AND indeed, considering that the Wisdom, Power and Goodness of the DEITY are such, as could not fail to enable and dispose Him to do all that was fit and necessary to conduct the Creatures which He had made (and would not desert) to that Happiness which was the End of their Being; I cannot doubt but that even the first Parents of Mankind, upon their first coming into Being, and in their State of Innocence, being then perfect Strangers to every Thing about them, and having every Thing to learn that related to their Well-being, must, in some Manner or other, have been taught by GOD himself, many Things relating to Food, Language, the Origin of Things, Philosophy and Religion, *&c.* (at least so much as was necessary for them to begin with) in order to their Well-being and Happiness. And when they had sinned against him, and fallen into a State of Mortality and Misery, it is natural to conclude, from the same Goodness and Compassion of the *Father of Mercies*, that he would take Pity of them, and teach them (what they could no otherwise know) in what Method, and upon what Terms, they should be pardoned and restored to his Favour, and how they should conduct for the Future, so as to be accepted with him, and restored to that Immortality which they had lost. All this is also very agreeable to the most ancient authentick Account we have of the Origin of Mankind.

§ 4. FROM

* Vide *Lactant.* L. III. C. 26, 27.

§ 4. FROM which Account rightly understood*, it appears, that as GOD had, very probably before the Fall, made the Garden of *Eden* an Emblem and Means of Inſtruction, both in Philoſophy and Religion, and explained his *neceſſary Exiſtence* and Perſonality in a *coeſſential Trinity*, ſignified by the divine Names, and repreſented by the *Sun* as an Emblem, in his threefold Condition of *Fire*, *Light* and *Spirit* (He being to the intellectual World analogous to what the Sun is to the Senſible) ſo it is no leſs probable that he ſet up the *Cherubims* with the *Flame* and *Sword* as Hieroglyphics or Emblems of the Goſpel, to teach Man, after the Fall, how to obtain Pardon, and regain the Immortality he had loſt, which was repreſented by the Tree of Life; by inſtructing Him, not only in the Knowledge of the *Trinity*, *Father*, *Son* and *Holy Ghoſt*, but alſo of the *Incarnation*, *Sacrifice*, *Satisfaction* and *Interceſſion* of the *Son* of GOD, in the Fulneſs of Time to appear as the *Inſtructor*, *Redeemer*, *Lord* and *Judge* of Mankind, and of the Preſence and Aſſiſtance of the *Spirit* of GOD for our Renovation and Sanctification. At leaſt this is certain, that *Sacrifice* muſt have been then inſtituted as an emblematical Means of Reconciliation, and Hopes were given of a glorious Perſon, who ſhould recover them from the Miſchief into which the Tempter had ſeduced them†; all which were doubtleſs much more particularly explained to them, than is accounted for

* Vide Mr. *Hutchinſon*'s Works, or Lord Chief Juſtice *Forbes*'s Thoughts concerning Religion, which deſerve to be well conſidered.

† Vide Biſhop *Sherlock* on Prophecy, and *Shuckford*'s Connection.

for in the very ſhort Hiſtory of the Fall; and no Account can be given how human Sacrifices, Polytheiſm and Idolatry could have obtained among Mankind, but upon Suppoſition of their being ſo many Corruptions of theſe original Emblems and Inſtructions, as Popery is of Chriſtianity. And as the Law of *Moſes* was, doubtleſs, a Revival of theſe original Symbols and Inſtructions, with Laws to guard againſt thoſe Corruptions; ſo GOD, by the Spirit of Prophecy, explained more and more in the following Ages the ſpiritual Meaning of thoſe Types, and the great Deſign He had in View, and had in ſome Meaſure diſcovered: And there manifeſtly appears, in the Whole, to have been one uniform conſiſtent Scheme carried on, from the Beginning downward, aiming all along at one End, *viz.* The Inſtruction and Reformation of Mankind; their Reſtoration to the divine Favour, and a ſincere and perſevering Obedience to the original Law of their Nature, finally to iſſue in their intire Perfection and Happineſs *.

§ 5. ACCORDINGLY (1.) we have abundant Evidence, both from Prophecy and Miracles, and undoubted Tradition ever ſince, That GOD (after ſuch a Series of introductory Inſtructions, Revelations and Inſtitutions from the Beginning) did at length ſend a glorious Perſon into our Nature, whom He declared to be His own SON, and who, being *truly GOD of GOD*, had inexpreſſible Glory with Him, even from Eternity, before the World was, being *the Brightneſs of His Glory, and the expreſs Image of His Perſon*, and by whom He viſibly diſplayed and exerted *His Almighty Wiſdom and Authority*, in the Creation

* Vide Biſhop *Butler*'s Analogy.

tion and Government of the World, and *in whom dwelt the Fulneſs of the Godhead* bodily in His incarnate State: This glorious Perſon GOD ſent among us, to act as a *Mediator* between Him and us: For as we are Sinners, it was very fit He ſhould treat with us by a Mediator; and as we are Men, it was no leſs proper, that He ſhould do it by one that ſhould appear in our own Nature, and converſe familiarly among us, that he might the better inſtruct us by his Example as well as his Precepts.

§ 6. AND (2.) as this was fit in itſelf, ſo accordingly the Fact was, That in His incarnate State, He abundantly proved by his Miracles, that He was indeed *a Teacher come from GOD*; and, being cloathed with divine Authority, He taught us all the great Principles of moral Truth and Duty, above demonſtrated, much more clearly than they had been generally known before, together with others meerly depending on Revelation and Inſtitution, relating to His Mediation and the New Covenant; and that in a Manner and Language, admirably ſuited to make the ſtrongeſt Impreſſions upon the Minds of Men, not only of the more thinking, but even of the general Rate and lower Sort of the human Kind; and enjoined them upon us, under the moſt weighty Sanctions, and affecting Conſiderations, as the Will and Law of GOD concerning us; and at the ſame time ſet us a moſt amiable Example, that *we ſhould follow His Steps.*

§ 7. AND (3.) as it was very neceſſary, that we ſhould be ſtrongly affected with a Senſe of the Heinouſneſs of Sin, as the moſt effectual Means to bring us to Repentance, and at the ſame time have ſufficient Security for Pardon, upon our Repentance

pentance

pentance, it pleased GOD to appoint that His blessed SON incarnate (freely submitting to it) should die for both these Purposes; that He should die for us, a *Sacrifice* for the Atonement of our Sins, and to set before us an Emblem of the Greatness of our Guilt, and the Heinousness of our Sins, in order the more effectually to induce us to repent of them, and forsake them; and to purchase and ascertain to us Pardon and Acceptance, upon our Repentance and Reformation; which merciful Purpose and Intention He had exhibited from the Beginning by the Institution of Sacrifices. Accordingly the blessed JESUS was graciously pleased to submit to a most painful and ignominious Death for our Sakes, *making His Soul an Offering for our Sins*, as the true Antitype of all the ancient Sacrifices (in which He had been exhibited, as the *Lamb slain from the Foundation of the World.*) And thereupon, in Virtue of the Right thereby acquired, He did, in GOD's Name, promise and ascertain, thro' His Merits and Mediation, *Pardon* to our sincere *Repentance* and *Faith* in Him, and the *Acceptance* of our faithful, tho' very weak Endeavours, to yield a constant and persevering Obedience to all His holy Laws for the Time to come.

§ 8. AND (4.) because of our great Weakness and Inability to repent, believe and obey, without GOD's Help, amid so many Temptations to the contrary; He hath also, for CHRIST's Sake, sent His *Holy* SPIRIT (by whom He hath always immediately exerted His *Almighty Will and Power*, in the Creation, Preservation and Government of the World) and promised His gracious *Assistance* to our ear-

nest

neſt Prayers and Endeavours, to enable us to withſtand the Temptations that lie in our Way, to mortify our Luſts and vicious Habits, and to comply with all the Duties incumbent upon us: Who, accordingly, is ever ready to aſſiſt us in all our honeſt and faithful Endeavours, and to render them effectual for the Renovation of our Souls, and to enable us to *bring forth Fruits meet for Repentance*, even all the Fruits of a ſincere, univerſal and perſevering Obedience to the Goſpel.

§ 9. And (5.) SINCE as Things now ſtand, we cannot have much elſe in View here, beſides a ſhort and uncertain Life, attended with many Calamities, and iſſuing in the *Death* or Diſſolution of our Bodies; and ſhould otherwiſe have been generally attended with much Darkneſs and Uncertainty about a future Life; CHRIST hath moreover, by his Sufferings and *Death* in our Behalf, taken away the Curſe and Sting of our Calamities and Diſſolution, and turned them into a Bleſſing, and made them a Means of promoting our greateſt Good; and hath by his triumphant *Reſurrection* and *Aſcenſion*, opened to us the glorious Views of a bleſſed *Immortality* both in Body and Soul, and aſcertained to us an *eternal Life* of unſpeakable Happineſs to be beſtowed upon us, in Conſequence of our final Perſeverance in Well-doing conformable to his Inſtructions.

§ 10. AND (6.) in the mean Time, and in order to qualify us therefor; as we could not, without Inſtruction from above, be well aſſured what *Worſhip* and Service would be acceptable to GOD, it was very needful that CHRIST ſhould teach us how to *worſhip* and adore him ac-

 ceptably,

ceptably, even *in Spirit and in Truth.* For as GOD hath been pleaſed to derive down all his Bleſſings and Favours to us thro' the Mediation of his *bleſſed Son*, and by the Influence of his *Holy Spirit*, ſo (as theſe Relations demand correſpondent Duties) it is fit, as he hath taught us, that all our Worſhip and Service, our Prayers and Praiſes, and all our Hopes of Acceptance, ſhould be offered up to Him, in Dependence on the Influence and Aſſiſtance of his Holy Spirit, and through the Merits and Mediation of his dear Son, who is the very *Truth (the Way, the Truth and the Life)* as the Condition of their obtaining Favour and Acceptance with him.

§ 11. AND (7, and *laſtly*) as every Thing that concerneth the Weal of Mankind is beſt promoted by ſocial Combinations; ſo GOD hath by his Son JESUS CHRIST, the great *Meſſenger of his Covenant*, appointed that we ſhould jointly combine and unite together in promoting our Happineſs; which is the great End of our Being, and particularly that we ſhould live in the conſtant Exerciſe of *ſocial Religion* for that Purpoſe. He hath therefore inſtituted *Baptiſm*, as a Rite of our Admiſſion into this Society, to repreſent and oblige us to all Purity and Holineſs in Heart and Life, and to ſeal to us the *great and precious Promiſes* of the Covenant of Grace, and the *holy Euchariſt*, as a further Means to ratify and confirm them, and to keep up in our Minds a lively Senſe of His Sufferings and Death, and of the mighty Obligations we are under, from His dying Love to us, to be faithful to Him who *died for us*, and *aroſe again*, and who is the great *Author and Finiſher of our Faith*; and moreover to perſevere in Love and Unity, as Brethren and

Fellow

Fellow Members of that holy Community of all good Men and Angels, whereof he is the Head and Lord. And as he would have us live in the constant Use of these Means for the promoting in us all the Virtues of a holy Life, which contribute to our final Happiness, he hath appointed an *Order* of *Men* to administer these sacred Rites, and to preside in the Exercise of this social Religion and Worship, and to explain and inculcate the *Divine Philosophy* which he hath taught us, in order to qualify and prepare us for that eternal Happiness which he hath provided and ascertained to us; so that we are to consider the Church and publick Worship as the School of CHRIST, wherein immortal Spirits cloath'd with Flesh, are to be trained and bred up as Candidates for eternal Glory.

§ 12. Now therefore, all those who do firmly believe all the great Truths of this *holy Religion*, whether *natural* or *revealed*, *i. e.* whether founded in Nature, or meerly depending on Revelation; and who under the Influence of them, do by *Faith* look for Assistance and Acceptance, only through his Mediation, and in the Method which he hath prescribed; and who, conformable to this holy Discipline of Christianity, do heartily *repent* and forsake their Sins, and return to their Duty, and faithfully live and act in all their Behaviour, both towards GOD and Man, from a Sense of Duty and Gratitude to GOD, their great Creator and Benefactor, and to JESUS CHRIST, their great Mediator, Law giver and Judge, and persevere in their Obedience, *faithful to the Death*. All these are said to be true *Christians*; and, even while they continue here, they belong to that heavenly Community which is called His *Kingdom*, whereof He is the Head, Lord and *King*, the great Vice-gerent of *GOD the Father*, and ſhall, through His Merits and Mediation, be accepted in Him, and be inconceivably happy with Him, in His glorious Kingdom in the Life to come.

FINIS.

Mr.

Mr. Wollaston's PRAYER, *R.N.* Page 120.

Somewhat Enlarged.

1. O THOU Almighty BEING, on whom dependeth the Existence of the World, and every Creature therein, and by whom all Things are governed and conducted to the several Ends of their Being, according to the various Natures which Thou hast given them: By whose good Providence I have been brought into Being, and most kindly preserved and provided for, from the Beginning of my Life to this Moment, and enjoyed many undeserved Advantages and Favours, with regard both to my Well-being in this Life, and my everlasting Happiness in the Life to come; and especially the inestimable Advantages of Thy Holy Gospel, made known to us in Thy Name, by Thy blessed Son Jesus Christ, and all that He hath taught, and done, and suffered for us; I beseech Thee graciously to accept of my most grateful Sense and Acknowledgment of all Thy Bounty and Beneficence towards me. *Bless* Jehovah, *O my Soul, and all that is within me, bless His holy Name: Bless* Jehovah, *O my Soul, and forget not all His Benefits: Who forgiveth all thine Iniquities, and healeth all thine Infirmities: Who redeemeth thy Life from Destruction, and crowneth thee with loving Kindness and tender Mercies! Bless* Jehovah, *O my Soul!*

2. And

2. And whereas, notwithſtanding the mighty Obligations of Thy Goodneſs, I have, in many Inſtances, ungratefully and perverſly ſinned againſt Thy moſt righteous and reaſonable Laws, in neglecting to do what Thou haſt commanded, and in doing what Thou haſt forbidden; I humbly profeſs before Thee, my utter Abhorrence of all my Perverſeneſs, and my ſerious Reſolution, by Thy Grace, to be more watchful againſt all Temptations, and to amend my Conduct for the Time to come. And I do moſt earneſtly beg the Forgiveneſs of my many Offences, through Thy infinite Mercies in Thy Son Jesus Christ, and that Thou wilt for His Sake, deliver me from the evil Conſequences of all my Tranſgreſſions and Follies. And I humbly beſeech the Aſſiſtance of Thy Holy Spirit, to endue me with ſuch Diſpoſitions and Powers, as may carry me innocently and ſafely through all future Trials; and to enable me upon all Occaſions, from a Senſe of Duty to Thee, my GOD, to behave myſelf conformable to Thy moſt holy Laws, which are indeed the Laws of Reaſon and Nature, in all Wiſdom, Probity and Virtue, and in the faithful Diſcharge of all the Duties of Temperance, Piety and Benevolence, with a humble Dependence upon thy infinite Wiſdom, Power and Goodneſs, and under a lively and habitual Senſe of thy All-ſeeing Eye, and the Account I am to give of myſelf to Thee.

3. I humbly beg Leave to commend both myſelf and mine to Thy moſt gracious Protection and Conduct, this Day, and at all Times: Suffer none of thy Creatures to injure us, no Misfortune to befal us, nor us to hurt ourſelves or others, by any Error or Miſconduct of our

own.

own. And vouchsafe us clear and distinct Apprehensions, and a right Judgment in all Things, together with all virtuous Tempers and Dispositions, and so much Health and Prosperity as may be truly good for us in this our present State of Probation. Grant that I may, at least, pass my Time in Peace, with Contentment and Tranquility of Mind; and, that having faithfully discharged my Duty to Thee, my GOD, to my Family and Friends, and to my Country and all Mankind, and endeavoured to improve myself in all virtuous Habits, and useful Knowledge, and done all the Good I could, throughout the whole Course of my Continuance in this World, I may, at last, calmly and decently take my Departure from this present Stage, and then happily find myself in a better State; even a State of unmixed and endless Happiness in the Life to come.

ALL which, and whatsoever else Thou seest needful for me and my Friends, and all Thy People, and for all Orders and Conditions of Mankind, and especially the Afflicted, I humbly beg, thro' the Merits and Mediation of Thy blessed Son JESUS CHRIST, comprehending them with myself, in that most excellent Form of Prayer which He hath taught us; *Our Father*, &c.

The END.

JE